ERIE TRAIL WEST

A Dream-Quest Adventure

Janie Lynn Panagopoulos

River Road Publications, Inc.

ISBN: 0-938682-43-1 Paperback
ISBN: 0-938682-35-0 Hardcover
Printed in the United States of America

Dedicated to the memory of my great-grandmother, Ada McCarty DeVoe, and my grandmothers Thelma DeVoe Critikos and Laura Kennedy Blount.

Contents

A Note from Janie Lynn Panagopoulos

Erie Trail West is based on extensive documentary research conducted in libraries, museums, and archives both in the Midwest and New York and on physical research along the remaining passages of the historic Erie Canal and locations in connection with the Toledo War.

The Erie Canal, a huge undertaking in its time, opened the western lands to immigration. It was a true corridor of expansion where people of many nationalities, skin colors, beliefs, lifestyles, and classes traveled and worked.

I have taken careful consideration to blend documented historical facts with a creative fictional story about the Erie Canal, the Toledo War, and the beginnings of Michigan statehood.

It is my hope this story will give its readers some insight into the lives of those people who came into the Great Lakes region by way of the canal—planting the seeds of settlements in a wilderness filled with unknown dangers and incredible hardships.

Thanks To—

Special thanks go to my friends who have allowed me to use their first names in the story: Jenny Lovett, Richard and Emma Chambers, Brendan Clark, and Kelly, Amanda, Shauna, and Krysta Grannis.

Also thanks to Patricia M. Van Skaik and the Public Library of Cincinnati and Hamilton County; Ellen M. Felser and the Erie Canal Museum, Syracuse, New York; Catherine L. Mason and the Buffalo and Erie County Historical Society; Michael A. Esposito, The New York State Library; the Lockport Museum, Lockport, New York; the Erie Canal Village interpreters, Rome, New York.

Lake Huron
Lake Michigan
Michigan Territory
Howell
Detroit
Lak
Indiana
Toledo
Ohio

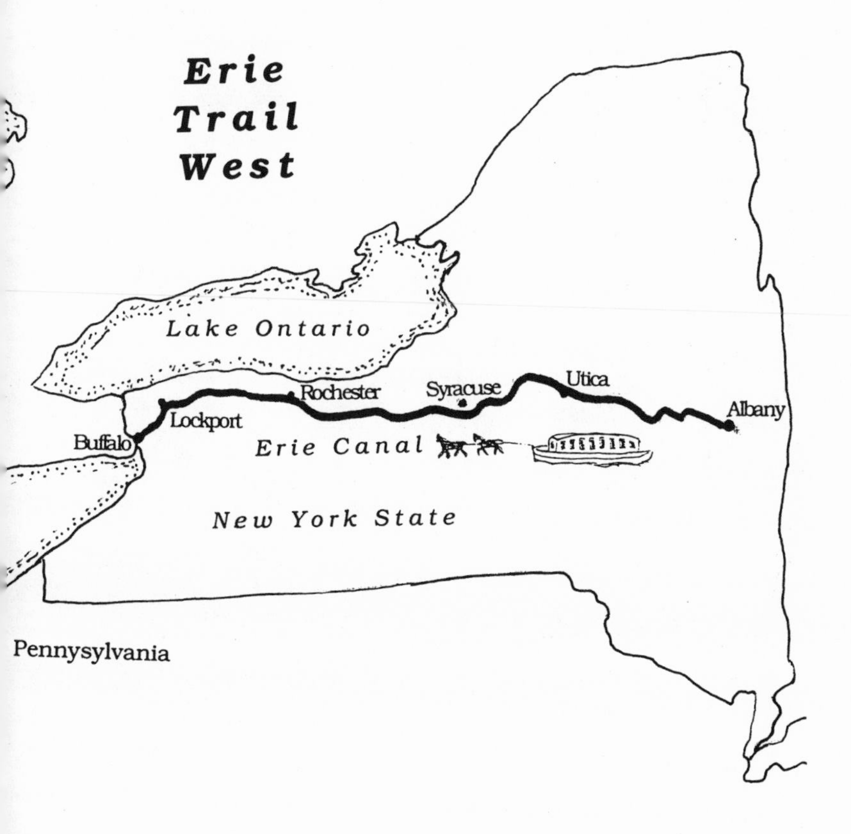
Erie
Trail
West
Lake Ontario
Rochester
Syracuse
Utica
Albany
Lockport
Buffalo
Erie Canal
New York State
Pennysylvania

Chapter 1
The Discovery

"Mom, why do I have to stay home? Doctor Kelly said I was fine."

"Doctor Kelly said you were doing just fine. As soon as all the scabs have healed you can go back to school. Chickenpox isn't anything to fool around with."

"Why do I have to have chickenpox? It's not fair. It's my birthday!

"Amanda, Krysta, and Shauna are going to be really upset when they find out you're keeping me home again today. I bet they have a surprise planned and everything. You're ruining it!"

"Jennifer, please. I'm trying to get ready for work.

"Daniel, give Jennifer her medicine. And please keep her occupied while I get ready.

"By the way, Jennifer," her mother continued, "I spoke with both Amanda's and Shauna's mother last night. Your friends do have a surprise for you. They're both home with the chickenpox, too.

"I promise, as soon as all your scabs are healed, you can take a special treat to school. And when everyone is feeling better you can have your birthday party. Is that a deal?"

"I guess so," said Jennifer as she hung her head and left the bathroom.

"Come on, birthday girl, let's get your medicine so that you can get better." Daniel Case put his arm around his daughter and smiled. "You know, after your mom goes to work, I'm planning on cleaning the attic. Since you seem to be feeling better, maybe you can help me. What do you think?"

"OK," Jennifer sighed. "I guess that's better than staying in bed all day.

"Daddy, I'm glad you don't work. At least you can stay home with me."

"Jennifer, you know I work. I just work at home so I can spend more time with both you and Mommy."

Jennifer grinned. She knew her father spent long hours writing newspaper articles and working on a book. She was proud her dad was an author.

"Can Sage come up, Daddy?"

"Yes, I guess we had better let that mutt up and get her fed."

Daniel opened the door to the basement and a brown and tan streak of energy bounded up the stairs and began running in circles around Jennifer and her father. Jennifer laughed and broke out of the circle with the dog chasing her.

"Jennifer," called her mother. "Settle that dog down! If she has eaten put her outdoors before she tears the house apart. You know a house is no place for a dog."

Jennifer looked up at her father who smiled and shrugged his shoulders. "I guess your mother's a cat person."

"Well, I'm not," said Jennifer loudly. "And I don't understand why Sage has to go in the basement or outside all the time."

Jennifer's father opened a can of dog food and emptied it into a bowl. Smelling the food, Sage raced into the kitchen and gulped it down.

"Look, you two," said her mother as she walked into the kitchen. "I don't want Jennifer to be playing around too much today. She still needs her rest.

"And besides, young lady, this is your birthday. I want you strong so you can open your gift when I get home from work. I think I'll pick up a pizza on my way home tonight. How does that sound?"

Jennifer gave her mother a hug. "Thanks, Mom."

"You get plenty of rest so you can go back to school soon."

Jennifer smiled as her mother gave her father a big kiss and started for the door.

"Don't forget to put that dog out when she's finished eating."

Sage looked up from her dish and cocked her head.

"Look!" said Jennifer, pointing to the dog. "She knew what you said. She's really smart."

"Well, when she's smart enough to stay off the furniture she can stay in the house more often," said her mother as she closed the door behind her.

"OK, young lady. We've all had our breakfast. Let's get started on the attic."

Jennifer ran upstairs to her room, putting on an old pair of jeans, a warm sweatshirt, and her tennis shoes. Jennifer liked going to the attic, but it was kind of spooky and dusty up there. I guess if I were over 150 years old my attic would be kind of spooky and dusty, too, she thought.

The house where Jennifer and her parents lived had been built in the 1800s by Jennifer's great-grandfather's great-grandfather. It had high ceilings and lots of rooms with **pocket doors**. It had belonged to the Case family ever since, and no one except the Cases had ever lived in it.

The door to the attic was in Jennifer's bedroom, inside the closet. When she was little she had worried that ghosts lived up there and might come down at night and get her. To ease her worry, Jennifer's father put a lock on the attic door and hung the key downstairs so that only he and Jennifer's mother could open it.

There was a soft knock on the bedroom door. "May I come in?" asked her father. "I want to get started on the attic."

Jennifer opened the door for her father who stood there with the key and a flashlight.

Mr. Case went into the closet and carefully pushed aside the clothes to unlock the attic door. "It's been awhile since I've been up here. I hope the spiders haven't made webs across the stairs again. I hate spiders. They give me the hebee-jeebees."

When Daniel turned the key and pushed the door open, cool stale air floated down from the attic. He shined the flashlight up the staircase, inspecting it for spider webs. "Looks good to me," he reported, and the two proceeded up the creaking wooden stairs.

Going to the attic, thought Jennifer, was like going back in time through a dark, dusty tunnel. All the things they used to use or needed to store from the past were in the attic. She spotted the scary black cat poster that hung in the front window at Halloween and the Christmas wreath that hung on the door each year.

Near the top of the steps Jennifer could see a dim light from the attic window. Her father snapped off the flashlight and grabbed the string that was attached to a light bulb over his head. With a quick snap, the bulb lit the attic with a bright light.

All around them were boxes piled as tall as Jennifer. The attic smelled like a dusty old book, and shadows filled every corner. As soon as Jennifer's eyes became accustomed to the new light, the shadows took form. There were old chairs, an old record player, and boxes of records. There was the highchair she had sat in as a baby.

Daniel Case walked along creaky old boards through a path of boxes, snapping on lights above him. "Jennifer, be sure to walk only on the boards and be careful not to slip. You might fall through the ceiling."

Jennifer had heard that warning from her father ever since she was old enough to come to the attic. It was funny, now that she was eleven, how he still thought he needed to tell her.

Jennifer saw her father opening boxes and looking inside. She peered around to see if she could find any boxes that belonged to her. There in a stack was a box marked "Jennifer's toys." Another read "Xmas tree lights," and still another was labeled "Dan's schoolbooks." Jennifer smiled to herself. This really is a time tunnel.

At the far end of the attic the sunlight pushed its way through a small, dingy window. As Jennifer made her way toward it, she found a rocking chair covered with dust and cobwebs.

"Daddy, is this the old rocker Mommy used to rock me in when I was a baby? The one that's so old that Grandma used to rock you in it?"

Daniel looked up from a record box he was searching through and smiled. "That rocker is even older than that. Your Grandma Case was rocked by her grandmother in it! Someday you might rock your babies in it, too."

"Oh, Daddy, you're weird."

Daniel laughed and went back to his records.

Jennifer tried to pick up an old cloth that lay in the shadows to dust off the rocker. As she pulled on the cloth, she found it was caught under the lid of an old trunk. She lifted the lid and realized the cloth was part of a large blanket.

"What's this?" Jennifer asked as she lifted the blanket. "It was in this old trunk."

Closing the record box, Daniel made his way to the far end of the attic. He smiled at his daughter's discovery. "Now, that's an old quilt and there's a story that goes with it."

Daniel took the quilt and shook out its many folds. Dust filled the air as it revealed its faded colors.

"Look here—can you read the date stitched into it?"

Jennifer traced her fingers over the stitching and read, "1837. Was this really made in 1837?"

"You bet it was. This was made by your—I guess it would be your great-grandmother's great-great-grandmother."

Jennifer looked closely at the stitches which were different lengths. Then she followed patterns of pink-flowered material that ran throughout the quilt.

"This is really neat."

"Check this," said her father. "There's more." From the trunk he pulled out a shaggy, old black fur robe with clumps of hair falling off it.

"Yuck, what's that? A bearskin?"

"No, but this is really neat. It's an old buffalo robe. It was used to cover your legs when you rode in a sleigh in the winter."

"Put it back. It's gross."

Daniel leaned over into the trunk and carefully folded the robe back into its place. Then he picked up several pieces of stone.

"Look at these," he said. "They're Indian arrowheads and a spearpoint. I remember sneaking up here when I was little and playing with these things. When my mother or my grandmother would miss me, they knew I was up here.

"My grandmother used to tell me that my red hair made me mischievous. Then she would sit me down and tell me stories about our family coming across the Erie Canal and into the Michigan Territory."

"The Erie Canal. Isn't that a big river or something? My teacher talked about that in school. You mean our family was on the canal?"

"You know, I think the old journal is still in here, too." Jennifer's father felt around under the robe. "Here it is." He pulled out an old black, leather-bound book with yellowed pages.

"This, Jennifer, is a very important book." He carefully opened it, revealing brown, faded writing.

"This is the story of your great-great-great-great-grandmother and our family when they first came into the Michigan Territory, into Livingston County."

"We live in Livingston County now. You mean, this is about our family when we first lived in the state of Michigan?"

"Well, when they came in 1836 it was still a territory. It wasn't until 1837 that Michigan became a state."

"1837. That's the date stitched in the quilt."

"You know, when I was about your age my grandmother showed me all these things and read the journal to me. I sat right here in this rocker. She put the old buffalo robe around me and read me the whole thing. Would you like to hear the journal, too?"

Jennifer realized how excited her father was and even though she knew the journal was important to him, she wasn't sure if she wanted to sit all morning listening to an old story.

"Come on. There are things in here that will surprise you."

"I don't have to have that dirty old buffalo robe on me, do I?"

Jennifer's father chuckled. "No, but how about the quilt?"

Sensing that this was important to her father, Jennifer finally agreed.

Daniel dusted off the rocker with his hand and spread the quilt on it. "Come on. You can cuddle up in this. Just imagine it's 1836 and you are traveling along the Erie Canal to the Michigan Territory."

Jennifer knew why her father was a writer. He had such an imagination. He could pretend he was any place doing anything he wanted. She sat in the chair and pulled the quilt around her.

As Daniel opened the old journal a piece of yellowed paper fell out. Jennifer rocked forward and picked it up. Carefully unfolding it, she saw it was an old piece of newspaper.

"It's a poem."

"No, those are words to an old song." Daniel took the clipping and cleared his throat.

"Please don't sing," said Jennifer, burying her head deep into the quilt.

"No, listen to this. This song is one reason so many people felt brave enough to take the Erie Canal and come to the Michigan Territory.

"There's the State of New York
where some are very rich; Themselves
and a few others have dug a mighty ditch
To render it more easy for us to find the
way,
and sail upon the waters to Michigan-i-a."

"Michigan-i-a?" asked Jennifer.

"Along the mighty Erie. . ."

"Daddy, please. No more. That's terrible."

"That, my dear, is *The Song of the Wolverines*. You get the idea anyway. The Erie Canal was something like a long ditch filled with water. It ran across the whole state of New York, from Albany to Buffalo—363 miles."

"I remember now. I learned a song in school about it." Jennifer began her song:

"I've got a mule, her name is Sal, fifteen
miles on the Erie Canal,
She's a good ol' worker and a good ol' pal,
fifteen miles on the Erie Canal.
We've hauled some barges in our day,
Filled with lumber, coal, and hay,
And we know every inch of the way from
Albany to Buffalo.
Low bridge, everybody down!
Low bridge, for we're coming to a town!

And you'll always know your neighbor,
You'll always know your pal,
If you've ever navigated on the Erie Canal.

"I remember that because my music teacher made our class get down on our knees when it came to 'low bridge.' That's how I remembered the Erie Canal. I thought it sounded familiar. I can't remember the rest of the song, but it was funny."

"And you made fun of my *Wolverine* song?"

Slipping the old clipping back into the journal, Jennifer's father began to read.

"It is July 6, 1836, two days after the great celebration of our American Independence."

Jennifer settled into the rocker and pulled the quilt around her.

Chapter 2
The Journal

My name is Jenny Lynn Case.

"Jenny Lynn Case?" said Jennifer sitting up straight in the rocker. "Jenny Lynn Case? That's my name. Daddy, you never told me I was named after someone special. Mom said it was a pretty name she liked."

"Well, it is a pretty name she liked, and it was also the name of one of your ancestors. That's the reason I liked it."

"This is really neat. You should have told me about this."

"Well, now it's a birthday surprise," said Daniel. "And by the way, my middle name, Richard, also comes from the journal. That was a surprise to me when I found out, too."

Just think, Jennifer thought to herself, I'm named after someone from a long time ago.

Her father continued to read.

I guess it might be said that our family, the Case family, was ***fiddle-footed****. All my life I heard stories of how we traveled to the colonies from England before the Tea Revolution.*

"The Tea Revolution," interrupted Daniel, "was actually the American Revolution. You see, a fight over taxes, including a tax on tea, led to the war."

Jennifer's father went back to the journal.

Our family first settled in Harteford-Towne, Connecticut, where the Case men were important people. Soon seeking more land, the Cases moved to New Jersey and not long after to Fulton County in New York.

Our family, now many, moved from place to place in New York. Papa met Mamma at a ***shucking dance*** *in the fall of 1823. They were married and settled twenty miles north of Utica, almost in the center of New York State.*

Jennifer's father looked up to see Jennifer staring back at him. Smiling, he broke the spell of the journal and asked, "What do you think?"

"I think it's great." She paused. "I'm named after someone in our family. I didn't know we were from England and I didn't know we traveled so much. No wonder I like it when we go on vacation. I just like to see new things. I'm like they were."

Jennifer's father smiled. "Yep. We come from a long line of travelers." He continued to read.

I was born in the winter of 1825. Our property was high and flat. There was so much land I couldn't see all of it, unless I stood on top of the chicken shed. I always got in trouble when I stood on the chicken shed, but I did it anyway because it was fun to see all the way to the woods.

I don't remember when Papa decided we would leave. It was very sudden. I believe he made plans without letting anyone know. I remember people passing our farm in their wagons. They would stop and tell stories about the territories across a huge lake called Erie.

One day a man came by with a map. I never saw a map so big before. But because I am a girl, I wasn't allowed at the table to look close-up at it. This was men's business, Mamma said. So I sat above them in the loft and looked down. I could see perfectly fine. The map showed a line drawn across the state of New York.

The man said, "This is the canal that connects us to the world." Then he drew his finger across New York to Lake Erie. That's where the canal got its name.

Then the man moved his finger over the lake to a place that looked like a mitten and said, "There it is,

Richard, the most pleasant place in the Territory. And the land is cheap."

"There's your name, Daddy," interrupted Jennifer. "Richard. Daniel Richard."

Jennifer's father nodded and continued on.

Papa and the man shook hands and slapped each other on the back. Mamma started rattling dishes on the table. She didn't even ask the man to stay for supper. I knew she was upset.

When the man left he said he would be by with the deed and book and would meet us "on the other side." On the other side. The words scared me. I thought maybe we were all going to die. When I asked Mamma, she agreed that was probably going to happen. When Papa heard her say that he got upset. It seems he sold our farm and planned for us to go to the "other side" of Lake Erie to the Michigan Territory.

That night Mamma cried and Papa puffed away on his pipe. I knew things were going to change. That is why I'm keeping this journal, so when I am old I will remember. And besides, Mamma used to be a teacher when she was fifteen and she said I need practice writing and this would be a good thing.

"Hey, sleepyhead. Do you want to go downstairs and lie down? We can finish this some other time."

"No, I'm awake. Keep reading. I like Jenny. She kind of sounds like me. You know you're always telling me I need help with my writing and spelling. Just keep reading."

It was two days later when the man came back. He was in a big wagon filled with boxes, children, and his skinny wife. He gave Papa a big book and a fancy paper with lots of writing on it. After that, Mamma started to fold and pack our things in boxes and trunks.

Shortly after Mamma got a letter. We don't get many letters because not many people know how to write and it costs lots of money to send a letter.

This letter was from Aunt Emma, Mamma's little sister. Mamma hasn't seen her in twelve years. Emma was only five when Mamma married Papa. Now she's seventeen and a married woman herself.

Waiting until you're seventeen to marry was popular in Mamma's family because Mamma was seventeen when she married Papa. Mamma was almost a **spinster**, *Papa used to say. Mamma always says she was just waiting for the right man, and besides, she was a teacher with important things to do.*

Aunt Emma also taught school until she met the right man. Now she's married a man who is captain of his own boat on the Erie Canal. The boat is called the "William and Mary." Papa has been in contact with Aunt Emma's husband and he says we will take this boat across New York on the Erie Canal all the way to Buffalo. At Buffalo we will ride a steamboat across Lake Erie to Toledo. Then, Papa says, we will buy a wagon and team and take our belongings to the Territory.

Even though Mamma wasn't happy about leaving the farm, she was pleased about seeing her sister again.

It didn't take long for us to pack. Papa packed his plow and bags of seed corn, rye, and wheat. He packed his tools and said he would, "build a new cabin that would reach the tallest trees."

Mamma packed her dishes, spinning wheel, broom, quilts, and all our clothes. She cried when Papa told her she couldn't take her mirror with the **gilded** *frame because it was too big. Mamma, being a smart woman, brought it anyway—packed in our big trunk filled with clothes so Papa wouldn't see it.*

The day before we left, I climbed to the top of the chicken shed and looked at the land and the woods that surrounded us. I knew I would never see this place again and it made me as sad as Mamma.

July 7, 1836

Last night Mamma and I slept under the wagon and Papa slept by the fire with his gun to watch for wolves and thieves. The woods around us had all sorts of animals. I had to squeeze my eyes shut really tight so I wouldn't see the eyes of owls in the trees.

We had bread and beans for breakfast. I got to walk along the trail beside the wagon. Mamma gave me her pink-flowered sunbonnet and told me to put it on. She said I was a young lady, soon to be of marriageable age, and no man would find me attractive if I had sun-dried skin. Papa laughed, but Mamma was serious.

It took us all day to finish the trip to Utica. I saw so many trees. I couldn't believe the Lord would have thought to make so many. I know now why our farm was such a good one. Our land was cleared and our fields were open like a prairie.

July 8, 1836

Last night we stayed at an inn in Utica. There were lots of people there. Some didn't even speak our language. Papa said they were Dutch or German.

There were even Indians who stood with their blankets pulled around them, talking quietly and smoking their pipes. I never have been afraid of Indians, because they were always my friends.

Once, when I was small, I decided to pick strawberries by myself. I knew I wasn't supposed to, but Mamma was churning butter and Papa was working in the fields. I loved strawberries, and being headstrong, I didn't want to wait.

I took the pail and walked into the woods. There I found an Indian man. When he realized I was looking for berries, he took me to the biggest patch I ever saw. We picked and filled my pail full and even ate some.

Soon Papa came running after me with his gun. He threw me over his shoulder and aimed his gun at my new friend. Papa shook me, saying I had scared the life out of Mamma.

The Indian offered his arm to Papa, because they shake arms—not hands like other folks do. After that he walked into the woods. He often came back to visit bringing berries for me and fish and meat for Mamma.

Indians don't scare me. They're a good group of people often misunderstood, Papa says.

I was never allowed to go off by myself again and got a good strapping for scaring Mamma like that. Of course, I wasn't supposed to climb on top of the chicken shed either, but I did that, too. Mamma always said I was headstrong, like Papa.

Jennifer, who sat half asleep in the rocker laughed at the bravery of her ancestor and thought she was really glad to have her name.

At the inn in Utica we shared a small room with one bed. The bed was only big enough for Mamma and me. Papa slept on the floor.

July 9, 1836

This morning we left early. As we passed the main hall I could see men sleeping in chairs and on the long table. The Indians were rolled up in their blankets and sleeping close to the fireplace.

Papa sold our wagon and horses and had our goods delivered to the docks. We began to walk to the far end of the docks where we were supposed to meet Aunt Emma and her husband.

Mamma made me put on my sunbonnet. She wore one, too. I don't know why she wears one. She's already married. I don't think Papa cares what her skin looks like.

Jennifer laughed. "I guess they didn't have any sunblock back then, did they?"

Daniel continued.

I had never seen so many people in my whole life. Mamma walked close to Papa and held my hand tight. We walked down a great road with buildings on each side. I smelled food cooking and remembered the good barley ***sop*** *we had at the inn the night before.*

Papa bought a hot loaf of bread for us to eat. Mamma warned him to let it cool before we ate it, so it wouldn't give us the ***belly wobbles****.*

We followed the road past a big mill to a dock where Momma spotted our belongings. The dock butted up to a big ditch filled with dirty brown water. In some places the ditch was lined with stone and in other places it was just dirt.

Papa said, "Well, my dears, this is Clinton's Big Ditch, or the Erie Canal. This canal is the future of all America. It connects the wild territories of the West to the civilized lands of the East."

Mamma interrupted and told him she wished he wouldn't use such words as "wild" and "civilized" because it might scare me. I knew these words scared Mamma. They only made me excited about our adventure.

Papa said the ditch would connect us to a rich new land where hundreds of bushels of corn grow on each acre and pigs grow fat ***rooting*** *for acorns in the* *forest. He said even the poorest families set their tables like a feast every day.*

I asked Papa why it was called Clinton's Ditch. He said it was named after the grand old governor of New York, DeWitt Clinton, who was elected in 1817. That was eight years before I was born.

When I asked Papa who built this great canal, he said men came from all over the world to work on it, especially from Ireland. The canal, he said, took so many workers because it was 363 miles long!

Then Papa sang me a song that got Mamma real upset. That's why I remember the words.

> *We are cutting a ditch through the gravel,*
> *Through the gravel across the state, by heck!*
> *We are cutting a ditch through the gravel,*
> *So the people and the freight can travel,*
> *Can travel across the state, by heck!*

Mamma grabbed Papa's arm and pulled it. I had never heard Papa use the word "heck" before, and now he said it twice, right out loud.

Jennifer had sunk down into the rocker with the quilt pulled high around her neck. Her eyes had closed and she no longer heard her father's voice.

Instead she saw a crowd of people on the docks. They gathered with their boxes, trunks, and **carpetbags** along the side of the canal. Young men called runners walked along the canal trying to convince travelers to board their boats.

Soon there was a blast of a horn. Coming up the canal was a long, narrow boat with a row of small windows on each side. Papa called this a packet boat.

This packet boat was painted all yellow and red like a pretty bird. The deck was almost flat with a small rail around it. On board there were rows of boxes, trunks, and carpetbags. Painted on the back in gold letters was the name, *Glory Be.*

On deck people waved to those along the canal. A man running along the canal with a handful of flowers almost bumped Mamma into the water. Everyone laughed and said the man was meeting his new wife. He had never seen her before, but she had answered his advertisement for a wife and was aboard the *Glory Be.*

"The bride is supposed to be wearing a pink ribbon on her bonnet," said the woman next to Jenny. "He is supposed to carry flowers. That way they will know each other."

Just then another boat painted bright blue pulled up along the canal. It, too, was loaded with people. When the people got off, another crowd got on. Even the lady beside Jenny left.

While Jenny waited, she looked for the lady with the pink ribbon on her bonnet and the man with the flowers. But she couldn't see them. The only one with a pink ribbon on her bonnet was an older woman. But Jenny didn't think she looked like a new bride.

As boats came and went, Jenny became more excited about the journey. She was sure the *William and Mary* would be a beautiful boat, too.

Mamma watched anxiously for Aunt Emma, while Papa paced back and forth. "Look," Papa pointed to a bunch of flowers floating in the canal. They looked like the ones the man was carrying for his new bride. Jenny wondered if the man had found his bride and decided not to claim her.

Just then a large man came down the towpath, whistling with his fingers in his mouth and shouting to everyone he passed. He had dirty brown hair and wore an old blue cap. He was the type of man who made Mamma nervous. "I wish those runners would leave us alone," she said.

As the man came closer Jenny could see that his once white shirt was stained with sweat and dirt and his pants were too short for his long legs.

He called loudly to Papa. "Could ya be the Case family?"

"Oh, dear Lord," said Mamma softly.

"Be nice," Papa whispered, "this might be your new brother-in-law." Papa was right.

Mamma smiled politely, but Jenny knew she was wondering why her sister would marry such a man.

"Follow me," said the man as he led them to an old dirty boat. Papa looked at Mamma and smiled, but Mamma swallowed hard.

Just then Aunt Emma called and waved from the deck. In a moment the sisters were in each other's arms.

It doesn't matter now if the boat looks like a pig boat, thought Jenny. Mamma and Aunt Emma are together again.

Aunt Emma turned to Jenny, squeezing her tightly and then looking her over carefully. Jenny felt as if she were a vegetable her aunt was about to purchase. "She has mother's eyes," Aunt Emma concluded. She squeezed Jenny again.

Then Aunt Emma turned to her husband, "This is Brendan Von Fleck McKee," she said with pride.

McKee took off his cap, bowed low, and kissed Mamma's hand. "I see where my wife gets her beauty. It must run in the family, madam."

Papa, who thought this odd, cleared his throat. His wife blushed.

McKee continued to introduce himself. "I was born along the canal. My father was a dirt digger from Ireland and me mother a German cook in the **dig camps** along the canal. I work the canal and plan to stay here 'til my dying day."

Mamma looked worriedly at Aunt Emma who quickly turned away and went below. Mamma hesitated and then followed.

McKee sent a **hoggee** or mule man to get the Case's supplies and soon they were all loaded on the deck. Papa worked quietly, straightening the boxes, barrels, and trunks. He wondered what to say to McKee who was the strangest man Papa had met in a long time.

As McKee prepared the boat to leave, a large woman called to him in German. He motioned for her to come aboard. She was followed by a boy who carried several canvas bags and a wooden box.

The woman spoke German to McKee and he spoke back. He even knocked the hat from the boy's head. Jenny decided that they knew each other.

With everyone aboard, the *William and Mary* was ready to depart. It was a long and narrow boat, about five feet above the water. At both the **bow** and **stern** there were steps leading down to a large cabin below. A long rope attached the bow of the boat to a team of mules up ahead on the **towpath**. The mules' job was to pull the boat along the canal.

Jenny watched as her Uncle McKee stood at the back of the boat and directed it to the center of the canal with a long-handled **tiller**. The boat glided forward on the muddy water. Jenny was surprised that such a big boat could move so easily.

"Watch this, **lassie**," Uncle McKee called to Jenny.

Up ahead was a low bridge. Jenny saw that her father was walking on the cargo, unaware of the bridge. She called to him just as the boat started under the bridge. As Papa looked up, the low bridge knocked his hat into the canal. Unhurt, he quickly jumped off the boxes to the deck.

McKee laughed and laughed. "Yankee farmers better beware until they get their canal legs," he called.

Upset with her uncle, Jenny went below. There she found her mother and aunt sitting in the prettiest red and white kitchen she'd ever seen. In the windows were bright, red and white checkered curtains tied back with red ribbons. All along the walls cooking supplies and dishes were neatly stacked on white painted shelves. To the right of the steps stood a new, shiny black cookstove.

"Come in, Jenny," said Emma, "and make yourself at home."

Jenny smiled at her aunt. The bright and cheery little kitchen was so different from the rest of the boat. At the far end of the kitchen a pretty flowered curtain hung in a doorway.

"Why don't you look around? Just go through the curtains."

Jenny pushed the first curtain aside and walked into a long room that was painted white. Seats were built against the walls under the windows. There were two unfinished tables in a corner with a saw and some lumber. There were also an old **bedstead** with a feather **tick** and some rolls of carpet. This must be where Aunt Emma and Uncle McKee sleep, Jenny thought.

Through a second curtain there was another room, small but brightly painted like the kitchen. There were also seats along the wall with red cloth cushions, a table with some books, and a writing desk, Hanging above the curtain was a painted sign that read "Gentlemen."

At the far end of the room was still another curtain. Pulling it back, Jenny could see a wash basin sitting on a small table. Above it was a small mirror and nearby a sign that read "Ladies." Everything was new and clean. It just didn't match the outside of the *William and Mary*.

When Jenny returned to the kitchen Aunt Emma smiled and asked, "Surprised? You see, when I met your uncle he was working aboard a beautiful packet boat. He wore a blue uniform and a blue cap with a gold braid. He was the handsomest man on the canal." Aunt Emma giggled and looked up at Mamma.

"He **courted** me awhile and then told me when he could afford a boat of his own, we'd be married. Well, one day we were out in a rented buggy, taking a Sunday ride when your uncle spied this abandoned boat on a **feeder creek**. She had been taken out of service because she was old. You see, the *William and Mary* hauled both passengers and freight, just like a stagecoach. That wears a boat out quickly.

"But Brendan thought the *William and Mary* was still sound enough to float and bought her for next to nothing. The next day we got married.

"That was just at the beginning of the shipping season in April this year. We've been fixing her up with the little money left from his savings. We're not quite ready to take on paying customers yet, but we haul freight and soon we'll have enough money to paint her outside. Then Brendan will put on his blue uniform and be a real captain. After that we'll buy us a mule team of our own or maybe two so we can pull day and night."

Mamma smiled because she knew Aunt Emma had a lot of faith in her husband.

"Did you see the low bridge as we left Utica? There'll be lots of them as we go, so be careful when you're on deck. You see, each farmer has a bridge crossing the canal to his property. The bridges are low because they're cheaper to build than high ones."

"Papa lost his hat in the canal on that bridge back there," Jenny blurted out.

"Papa lost his hat?" Mamma asked.

"And I suppose my husband laughed at him, too. You see, he has a peculiar sense of humor when it comes to bridges. One day when we were just married I had taken an afternoon to boil up settlement water and scrub clothes.

"You can't wash often with the muddy old water from the canal or it will stain your clothes. Like the shirt your uncle has on today. I washed it just last week in canal water and it looks like he's worn it for months!

"Anyway, when I finished washing I stacked freight boxes to string a line for the wash to dry on the deck. I didn't know you were supposed to use a pole line so you could lower it. Then along came one of those low bridges and scooped my wash right into the canal along with some freight boxes."

"Oh, Emmy!" Mamma cringed at the idea of all her sister's hard work going into the muddy canal. "You got the clothes back, didn't you?"

"Brendan was so busy fishing out the freight that he paid no never mind to the clothes. A boat came the other way and caught the line, pulling it up the canal a ways with my clothes.

"The hoggee, bless him, tied the mules and ran back and fished out the clothes. He told me there was a small boy standing on that bridge waving my **drawers** in his hand and laughing.

"But the hoggee didn't go back for them because he was embarrassed. He thought it was too personal a thing for a man like him to carry."

Mamma's eyes and mouth popped open in shock. Aunt Emma looked at her and burst into laughter.

"Aunt Emma, that's a great story," said Jenny, joining the fun.

Mamma thought the story wasn't so funny, but smiled and shook her head as she began snapping string beans for supper.

When Jenny went back on deck, she tried to imagine how the *William and Mary* would look with a new coat of paint. She wondered how Uncle McKee would look in his blue uniform with gold braid on his hat.

Papa stood talking with Uncle McKee who held the tiller and steered a straight, smooth course along the center of the canal. In front of the boat were the two mules, hitched one behind the other, pulling the boat on a long towline. The hoggee walked behind them, slapping their backs with a whip to keep them moving along the towpath. Beside the path the tall grass swayed back and forth as if there were some unknown creature hiding there.

Down in the kitchen Jenny heard the German woman talking loudly. She also spoke English, but she had a very thick accent and was hard to understand. The boy who had boarded with her came up on the deck. He walked by Jenny, giving her a sneer and sticking his nose in the air. Jenny wanted to stick out her tongue at him, but she knew if Papa saw her he would not approve.

The boy walked right up beside Papa and Uncle McKee and was welcomed into the conversation. Soon, Uncle McKee let him take the tiller and steer the boat. The boy's round face beamed with pride.

It isn't fair being born a girl, thought Jenny. Boys always get to do things that are more fun. She pulled down her sunbonnet as the boat passed under another low bridge. This time, Papa ducked. Her uncle laughed and slapped him on the back.

Along the towpath Jenny watched the grass dance and move. Again it seemed as if something was there. Just at that moment the boy pushed his way past Jenny and ran below. When he returned he carried a gun. Mamma, Aunt Emma, and the German woman followed him up on deck.

Pointing toward shore Uncle McKee shouted to the hoggee. "Beware. There is some critter following along in the woods. It might be a panther." Everyone watched carefully, but the grass and leaves were still.

The German woman began to speak excitedly in her accent. "Ven I live in Territory of Michigan der vere lots of volves and panthers. Too many volves; too many panthers; too many Indians. I come back to New York so to live in civilization."

Seeing the worried look on Mamma's face, Jenny knew she didn't like the idea of leaving civilization.

The young German boy began hopping around the deck, pretending to shoot the gun. His mother laughed when he said, "Ah, Mamma, I kill de volves for you."

By evening the *William and Mary* had passed many small villages and went under too many low bridges to keep count. Near the villages were large fields of corn, wheat, and barley. But each time the boat moved away from the settlements there were only dark, tangled woods.

That evening the passengers ate supper in the kitchen. Jenny sat between Mamma and Papa so she didn't have to sit beside the boy. When it got dark, the boat pulled up along the edge of the canal and stopped for the night.

"Lots of boats pull late into the night," said Aunt Emma. "We stop because we rent our mules at public horse stations along the way. Two mules and a hoggee will pull for six hours and then another set will pull. Some boats even have a second crew at the tiller. But not ours. There is only one man who runs the *William and Mary*."

Uncle McKee slipped his arm around Aunt Emma and gave her a squeeze.

That night Mamma lit an oil lamp and led Jenny around the deck to the front stairs and the cabin marked "Ladies."

The yellowish light from the lamp showed that a set of seats were now packed away. A row of three narrow beds—an upper, a middle, and a lower—now hung in their place. The beds looked like cots and were only far enough apart to crawl between.

"Papa and the German boy will sleep in the men's quarters," whispered Mamma. "And Aunt Emma and Uncle McKee have their own bed."

Mamma whispered because the German woman had already gone to bed. She had chosen the center cot.

"I don't want to climb to the top. What if I fall?" said Jenny.

"Sleep on the bottom," whispered Mamma. "I''ll be spending the evening with Aunt Emma. We have sewing to do.

"Take off your shoes, skirts, and **blouson**, and leave on your **shift**." Mamma handed Jenny a blanket.

Jenny had never slept in her shift before. At home Mamma thought this was uncivilized.

Crawling into the lower cot, Jenny was soon uncomfortable. The cot was only a piece of canvas stretched over a wooden frame. There was no feather tick like hers at home. The pillow was so small, she decided, it was dishonest to call it one.

"Lie still down there," whispered Mamma as she left the cabin. Jenny watched as the shadows from the lamp danced across the windows.

The cot occupied by the woman above sagged with her weight. Rolling over, Jenny accidentally jabbed the woman with her elbow. The woman rolled over, too, and then came an uproar of snoring. It started with a snort, then a whistle, followed by a grunt. For a moment there was silence, and then it started over again.

Jenny could hardly keep from giggling. If jabbing the sleeping woman made her snore, Jenny thought, maybe jabbing her again would make her stop. She raised her elbow and gave the woman a sharp poke. Then she held her breath as the woman moaned and rolled over once again. Soon it was silent, but the woman's new position created a bulge in the cot that nearly rested on Jenny's shoulder.

Jenny did not dare move. Lying perfectly still she listened to the soft breathing that now came from the woman above her. In the background a lone wolf howled sadly from the woods, and Jenny slowly drifted off to sleep on her cot along the great Erie Canal.

Chapter 3
Montezuma Swamp Boy

Early the next morning Jenny awoke to a suffocating feeling she had never felt before. Blinking her eyes open in the twilight she could see that the canvas on the cot above her had ripped. Part of the woman above her now hung through the hole and rested on top of her.

Startled, Jenny squirmed free and rolled out onto the floor. She hoped the woman wasn't going all the way to Buffalo.

On the window seats that had not been made into cots, Mamma lay wrapped in a blanket. That's a hard bed, thought Jenny, but at least she didn't have to worry about getting squished.

The cool morning air made Jenny shiver and she pulled her blanket from the cot, wrapping up in it. Just then she heard a strange noise from the deck above. Sliding open the door at the top of the stairs, Jenny crept outside.

Looking toward the back of the boat, Jenny could see the canal covered with a thick, gray mist. The sun was just starting to rise above the treeline. As she turned toward the front of the boat, she saw something move. Quietly moving closer she saw someone prying the lid off one of the supply boxes. Just then a red-headed boy stood abruptly and turned toward her. "I ain't stealing," the boy defended himself. "I'm just hungry."

As soon as he had spoken the boy turned and jumped from the boat to the canal bank. Waiting for him along the bank was a large dog. The two of them ran off, breaking through the brush to make their escape into the woods.

"Jenny! Jenny!" a sharp voice half whispered. "Get yourself down here and dress." It was Mamma. "Young lady, you will not parade around half-dressed like an uncivilized girl. Come below!" she demanded.

That morning after the boat was hitched to a fresh team of mules, Jenny went back to the deck and watched the path, looking for the red-headed boy and his dog. As she stood there, the German boy pushed his way past her, acting as if she were invisible. Some people, thought Jenny, just don't have any manners.

Speaking to Uncle McKee in what Jenny thought was a very whiny voice, the boy soon got what he wanted. The *William and Mary* came close to the bank, allowing him to jump off. He began running and skipping along the towpath, picking up stones and throwing them into the water. Boys have all the fun, thought Jenny, wishing she could join him.

Soon from up along the path came the voice of the hoggee. "Lock be-looow. Steady as she goes."

Uncle McKee put a tin horn to his lips and a shrill note sounded down the canal. Then in the distance came the clinking of a chain. "We're moving into the locks," called Uncle McKee loudly.

Ahead was a narrow passage between two high walls of stone. A man, waving one hand at Uncle McKee, turned a crank with the other. The *William and Mary* headed into the passage toward two great wooden gates that closed off the canal.

Frightened, Jenny looked around for her father. The lock was only a little larger than the boat, and beyond the great wooden doors Jenny saw water standing much higher than it was in the lock.

The *William and Mary* bumped against the side of the stone wall. Uncle McKee, pressing a pedal with his foot, released the **towline**. The hoggee urged the mules forward and pulled the line up onto the bank. Uncle McKee tossed other lines to lock attendants standing above them along the stone walls.

As soon as the boat was secure the lockkeeper turned a crank to wind up an iron chain which pulled two large wooden doors closed behind them. He then opened the flood gates in the lock with an iron lever. Water bubbled and foamed around them while gushing sounds filled the air.

As the water rose, so did the *William and Mary*. Soon it was level with the water beyond the front wooden gates. The attendants untied the boat from the wall while the lockkeeper cranked the gates open ahead. Uncle McKee and the hoggee hooked up the towline and the boat was soon on its way again.

Shortly after, Jenny saw the red-haired boy and his dog between the woods and the towpath. As the hoggee yelled at the pair, the German boy scooped up mule dung and hurled it at them.

The boy and his dog raced for the woods while the German boy scrambled to find a rock. This time he hit his mark, and the dog yelped and disappeared into the woods. The German boy laughed and waved his arms in victory. Grinning, Uncle McKee steered the boat close to the bank so that the boy could hop aboard.

Shocked at the boy's behavior, Jenny marched up and demanded, "What's your name?"

The boy's eyes opened wide in surprise. "I'm Hermann Gustov. That was funny, ya?"

"That was not funny! You are the meanest, rudest boy I have ever met. If I were your mother, I'd. . .."

"Now wait a minute, missy," called Uncle McKee from the tiller. "You ain't his mother so you be tendin' to your own **knitting**."

Jenny couldn't believe what she had heard. Her uncle was standing up for that Hermann Gustov! She put her hands on her hips and stomped away.

Hermann followed. "You know de boy is no good. He was raised by a vitch. You see his hair? It is red. Dat is a sign of a vitch, too. His animal is a verevolf.

"In swamps de ghosts and spirits of de dead take girls and boys right off de towpath. You can hear de verevolfs call at night too. Da boy can cast spells and do harm. I only try to help."

Jenny could see that Hermann was serious, but she had never heard such an outlandish story in all her life. Angrily she stomped down the steps to report all this to her mother. On her way down she ran into the German woman who had her arms full of items, including the ripped canvas cot. She smiled shyly at Jenny and pushed her way up the stairs.

"Mamma!" Jenny called loudly as she entered the kitchen. "That Hermann boy. . .."

"Jenny," her mother said sharply, "a young lady does not enter a room with a loud voice."

"Sorry, Mamma."

"You must have had quite a night," interrupted her aunt. "Mrs. Gustov, Brendan's aunt, is going to take the cot home and repair the canvas. She was so embarrassed. "

Hermann is Uncle McKee's cousin? No wonder he is sticking up for him, thought Jenny.

"Jenny, I would like you to practice your stitching on these quilt squares." Jenny's mother set a basket filled with quilting squares, thread, and needles on the table. "Sewing is very important if you hope to marry someday. And besides, we need to make a baby quilt for Aunt Emma."

"Aunt Emma is going to have a baby?" Jenny exclaimed in surprise.

"Shhh. It's still a surprise for your uncle." Mamma smiled and began working on the squares.

Just then Jenny felt the boat slow. It bumped up to the side of the canal and came to a halt.

"Mrs. Gustov and Hermann are leaving. We need to say goodbye," said Emma starting up the stairs.

Jenny wasn't going to say goodbye. She wanted to say "good riddance." And she bet that Hermann didn't even know about Aunt Emma's baby!

Emma and Mamma handed Mrs. Gustov's bundles to her and Hermann along the bank. Soon a squeaky wagon came from a path in the woods. Its driver was an old man with a long beard and straw hat. He smiled and waved at McKee who called and waved back. With much effort, the man stopped the horses and crawled down from the seat.

Speaking German, the old man and Uncle McKee laughed and joked together. Meanwhile Hermann loaded the wagon and turned the team of horses around so they could return to the path in the woods. Jenny watched and thought perhaps it wasn't all fun being a boy, especially if you were like Hermann.

When Mrs. Gustov climbed aboard the wagon, it tilted with her weight. The old man pulled the reins and slapped the horses' backs as the family disappeared into the woods. Uncle McKee told Papa he couldn't believe his aunt would live in those woods, where "ten mosquitoes weighed a pound."

Uncle McKee saw Jenny listening and smiled. "Ya know, lassie, there is no sense getting worked up over Hermann. He's ignorant, that one, and his head is filled with superstitions. He's heard old German stories that would scare a ghost. I know. I heard 'em all when I was a boy."

"But he said," insisted Jenny, "that the boy on the path was a witch and was raised by a witch and his dog was a werewolf!"

"They're just stories, girlie. You see when the ditch was dug through here, there were lots of swamps along the canal path. Lots of men lost their lives from **malaria** and **ague**.

"The children of those men were often abandoned by their mothers who had no money to feed them. The mothers couldn't bear to watch them die slowly by starvin'. So they left 'em, hoping someone would come along and take 'em in. Often times the Indians would adopt them into their families.

"Sometimes even workers would bring the poor things home. When I was a boy, me **da** brought home a babe. She was one he found along the canal. She died shortly after, but we loved her like **kin**.

"The red-haired boy ya saw was one like that, only he was raised by an African **runaway**. A slave woman from North Carolina, they say. The woman made her way here to New York across the mountains. She was afraid of being found, so she lived in the swamps of Montezuma west of here. She found the boy, so I've been told. Her own babes had been sold as slaves, so she raised him 'til he was able to hunt and grub for both of them."

Jenny listened to the story and thought how sad it would be to be sold as a slave or be abandoned by your mother and have to live in a swamp.

"That wolf of his, however, is another story. Any wolf is a devil at heart."

"It isn't a wolf, it's just a big dog," insisted Jenny.

"I never saw a dog with the brown and tan markings of a wolf that wasn't one."

"But it's the boy's friend, maybe his only friend," said Jenny sadly.

"Be that as it may, I could use the ten dollars its hide would bring to help me paint the boat. You see, missy, you have the soft heart of a woman and that's why the woods are so hard on your kind."

Jenny stood silent, not knowing what to say. It was obvious to her that he liked boys better than girls.

Walking to the front of the boat, Jenny watched the towpath as they came to another stable and changed mules. Her father joined her. "I don't want you to pay any attention to your uncle. He's a rough sort of fellow, but he means well. Just respect him and the two of you will get along fine. Underneath he has a big heart, and your aunt loves him, at least, that's what your mamma says."

Looking at Papa, Jenny knew this trip was hard on him, too.

Soon the canal came to the Seneca River and a long **aqueduct**.

"See the aqueduct, Jenny," said Papa as he pointed ahead. Jenny saw something that looked like a bridge over the river. Only this bridge was filled with water to carry the canalboats across the Seneca. She watched as the *William and Mary* easily glided along the aqueduct, pulled by the mules on a special pathway.

"After this," Uncle McKee called out, "we'll be passing through the Canton Valley which is halfway between Albany and Buffalo."

Now off the aqueduct, Jenny could see someone carrying a long stick. As the boat moved on, Jenny could see red hair. It was the boy again.

"Missy, run below and ask your aunt for food for the boy's bundle. This is how the orphans do it. They pass a stick bundle over to us, and we put what food we can in it for them to eat."

Running quietly to the kitchen so Mamma wouldn't notice her and make her stay below and quilt, Jenny thought about how brave or hungry the boy must be to come back again after what Hermann had done.

Jenny's aunt gave her a link of sausage and a half loaf of bread. "That should do him for now," she said with a smile.

Hurrying back upstairs, she found that Uncle McKee no longer stood at the tiller. Instead he held a gun to his shoulder and aimed down the path at a dog.

Frantically Jenny yanked off her bonnet, shoved the food inside, and heaved it to the path. Then, with all her strength, she pushed Uncle McKee, throwing him off balance. The gun discharged into the air with a blast and a puff of smoke.

Not knowing what was happening, the boy grabbed the bonnet and ran back into the woods, his dog at his heels.

"Gol blast ya, girl! What in tarnation had you a mind to do? Didn't ya hear a word I said before about money for that wolf pelt?"

By this time Papa, Mamma, and Aunt Emma had all gathered on the deck where Uncle McKee was pacing like an angry cat. "That girl of yours, Mr. Case, is a spitting panther. A nasty wildcat she is. She has no woods' sense and the wilderness ain't no place to be takin' her.

"I explained to her, nice as I could, about the wolf pelt and the money, but she has no sense in that head of hers."

Papa stepped up to McKee, but Mamma quickly pushed him aside as she stepped between the two men.

"I would appreciate it, Mr. McKee, if you spoke about my daughter in a civilized manner. She was not raised on a boat, in a swamp, or along a canal. She is a smart girl and a good girl and you, sir, go out of your way to be rude.

"I have been tried by you, sir, and I—." Mamma's strength broke and tears came to her eyes. Aunt Emma put her arms around Mamma and started to escort her below. Turning sharply to her husband she called, "Husband, you are a brute."

Jenny followed Mamma below. Papa stayed on deck trying to mend the rip she had caused in the family .

That afternoon and evening Jenny washed dishes, peeled potatoes, swept floors, and worked with Mamma on the baby quilt. Aunt Emma apologized for her husband and tried to explain his temper and the way of the canal.

Along toward evening Uncle McKee called for Jenny to come to the deck. "Girlie," he said looking at Jenny, "I beg forgiveness for this day, but ya have to learn to leave men's business alone.

"Am I forgiven?" he asked as he removed his dirty cap from his equally dirty head.

Jenny knew Aunt Emma made him say this but she accepted. He reached down and kissed her cheek gently. "That seals it now," he said with a smile.

"I want ya to watch this packet boat comin' up ahead. It's the *Whirlwind* and she has a regular schedule like a stagecoach. Since she carries only passengers, she's light on water. Her nose is sharp, too, and she cuts the water fast. She can pass us like we aren't movin'. You'll hear her horn in a minute."

Papa came to stand beside Jenny and whispered, "Everything better?" Jenny nodded and watched the *Whirlwind* approach.

"How fast is she coming, McKee?" Papa asked.

"Well, we be movin' about three or four miles an hour, and she's probably goin' five. Too fast for the canal because at speeds like that her wake washes out the banks. It's a dangerous thing. Still, if a packet comes up behind a line or freight boat, we must let it pass. It's the law."

Just then a horn blast from the *Whirlwind* was heard. The *William and Mary* glided to the right side of the canal. The hoggee pulled his mules off the path. Then he backed them up so that the towline became slack and lay on the ground. The team pulling the packetboat stepped over the line, passing the *William and Mary's* hoggee and mules.

The section of the towline which draped across the canal dropped below the surface of the water. Soon the *Whirlwind* made its way over the sunken line, between the bank and the *William and Mary*.

Jenny could hear the sound of the line rubbing against the bottom of the packet boat."What if the line gets tangled?" she asked her uncle.

"Don't be sayin' that, missy," Uncle McKee responded quickly. "I've seen teams of mules and horses pulled off into the canal and men and women yanked from the decks and drowned by tangled lines.

"See here," Uncle McKee held up a long, curved knife. "It's the captain's job to cut any lines that cross or endanger boats or teams. And it's a sad day when the lines have to be cut. They're costly, and it takes time to repair 'em."

Jenny watched as the *Whirlwind* moved past them. Just then a tall man with a great curling mustache appeared along the bank. He waved his arms high in the air, motioning for McKee to take him aboard.

Aunt Emma called up from the kitchen. "It's meal time, so that must be the canal superintendent with some urgent news that gets him invited to supper."

"Hush, woman," came Uncle McKee's voice as he turned the bow of the boat to the bank. The old man hopped aboard, shaking hands with Papa and slapping Uncle McKee on the back. He seemed to be right at home.

When the boat stopped for the evening and the team was released, everyone went below for dinner. Aunt Emma dished out steaming bowls of stew and put out fresh bread. The men talked as they ate.

"I heard it told you were duck hunting from the *William and Mary*, McKee," he said with a glint in his eye. "Ya know it's my job to control such nonsense along this stretch of the canal. That could be a dangerous sport with all them **emigrants** traveling about here."

Uncle McKee glanced quickly at Jenny before responding to the superintendent. "Well, there was a wolf along the towpath followin' a beggar boy. I thought the boy might be in danger, so I took aim and slipped. The gun went off into the air."

"That boy," said the superintendent as he wiped the crumbs from his mouth with the back of his hand, "that boy wouldn't have happened to have red hair, would he?"

"As red as fire. He's the old witch's boy."

Surprised by what her uncle had said, Jenny was equally surprised that the old man knew exactly who he meant.

"Now, McKee, that boy is not really a witch's boy. Since when did you start believing things like that? That there young'un is one of those orphans raised in the swamp by that African runaway."

"You mean that poor boy was abandoned?" asked Mamma.

The superintendent nodded. "You know ma'am, it's been only a few years since that **cholera epidemic** followed along the canal and left many children orphans. Some starved and died. Others just disappeared into the woods and swamps and weren't never heard from again.

"No one wanted this boy with red hair 'cause people hereabouts are superstitious. It wasn't until that African runaway found him that he was rescued. She thought his red hair would bring her luck. Raised him back up in Montezuma Swamps, a few miles up the canal from here."

"Such a sad story," said Mamma.

"Sad but true, ma'am. You should be watching the cholera, too. Why, in 1834 it swept through the Michigan Territory leaving a trail of death behind. That was just two years ago."

Mamma's eyes widened and she got up to clear the table.

"The reason I stopped to let you know, McKee, that boy you shot at. . .."

"I didn't go shootin' at no boy," McKee protested.

"Well, anyway, that boy was caught this afternoon stealing taters off a freight boat up the canal a piece. I ran him into the poorhouse in the settlement, so he won't be bothering you no more."

"What about the wolf?" asked McKee.

"No wolf, no. Just a scrawny red-haired boy. But thanks for telling me. Wolf pelts are bringing ten dollars cash money. I'd like to get in on that deal."

"Speaking 'bout deals, Mr. Case, seeing your wife ain't partial to epidemics, you might want to consider settling south of the Erie along Ohio way. Michigan Territory might be too rough for ya, seeing you ain't got no sons to help clear the land. I've seen more than one strong man broken for want of an extra pair of hands to work the land."

Mamma, who was washing dishes, wiped her hands on her apron and stood listening.

"The reason I say this is 'cause I just happened on a piece—by luck have you—of prime land. Sixty acres along the Maumee River. I could let you have it, for say, four hundred dollars."

"By luck you say," interrupted McKee. "You mean you stole it in a card game from some honest farmer."

"It was an honest game, McKee."

Mamma, totally disgusted, went back to the dishes and Papa chuckled to himself.

"Sir, are you trying to sell me land for more than six dollars an acre?"

"It's cleared land. That's fair. It's also along the Maumee in a real state to boot, sir."

"I just bought 160 acres of prime land in the Territory and only paid $240. And I heard say Michigan will be a state in no time."

Mamma looked up in surprise and listened.

"The land is **second land,** and it has twenty acres cleared. The rest is hardwoods with a sugaring camp. There's even a cabin and good water."

"I hope for your wife and daughter's sake that is so. I have heard it told ya can't trust a Yankee land **speculator**."

"This Yankee speculator is a friend, sir, and will be my neighbor with his family in the Territory. He came by the land honestly after the death of his brother." Papa's voice started to rise.

"Now see what I was telling you about the cholera epidemic? It's dangerous in the Territory."

"The brother died of old age, and I would thank you not to be upsetting my wife with all this nonsense. And as for not having sons, my daughter is a strong, healthy, headstrong girl, and I'm proud of it. And for the future, you can never tell what the Good Lord will bring your way."

With that Papa stood up and pulled the napkin from his neck and tossed it on the table. He excused himself and went up the cabin stairs. Jenny had never heard Papa talk so loud or say he was proud of her being headstrong like himself.

Mamma and Aunt Emma banged the dishes around for a while and Uncle McKee filled his bowl and ate some more stew in silence.

The superintendent soon stood to leave. "Well, I suppose you good folks have entertained me enough for this evening. I'll be on my way. By the way, McKee, no duck hunting off your boat or next time I'll have to fine you." Picking his teeth with his dirty fingernail, he walked slowly up the stairs and climbed off the boat.

"No duck hunting or he'll fine you," said Aunt Emma. "That miserable, old goggle-eyed snapping turtle. And trying to scare you all into buying land he cheated someone out of. The nerve of that man!"

"All right, woman, let's have some peace this evening. It's been a trying day," said McKee.

Aunt Emma shook her head in surprise as Uncle McKee finished his meal.

When she was done with the dishes, Mamma joined Papa on the boxes at the front of the boat as he smoked his pipe. Jenny watched as Mamma took Papa's hand and smiled. She knew her mother was proud of the way her father had stood up to the superintendent. She guessed that Mamma was also happy to hear Papa describe their new home as a wonderful place.

That night Jenny slept on a center cot by a window. Aunt Emma even pried the painted window open so she could look out and smell the cool night air. A light breeze blew, gently rocking the boat on the canal. In the distance, Jenny again heard the lonely cry of a wolf-dog in the forest.

Chapter 4
An Extra Pair of Hands

The next morning was bright and sunny and Papa was in a very good mood. After breakfast he asked Jenny if she would like to walk with him to the next village.

When Mamma heard his plans she didn't like them one bit. "The girl has no bonnet, and the sun isn't good for her."

"Don't be worrying so about her. I'll find a place with **dry goods.** They'll have girls' bonnets. I might even bring you back a surprise," he said to Mamma with a smile.

They left the *William and Mary* before the hoggee arrived. Uncle McKee had promised to meet them along the canal docks where he was going to be picking up freight to be carried to Buffalo.

The walk along the path felt good to Jenny. The air was warming and the small patches of mist along the canal disappeared into the sunshine like little ghosts.

As he walked, Papa sang his "by heck" song right out loud. He told Jenny not to tell Mamma and let it be their secret.

The next settlement was only two miles up the canal. As they drew closer there was more and more cleared land. Numerous low bridges crossed over the canal telling them that there were many farms in the surrounding area.

Once in the village, Jenny and her father made their way to the village square. There was a board with many announcements posted on it. Mr. Case quickly scanned the notices. There were farms for sale and rewards offered for runaway slaves. One notice told about a **vendue** that was to be held that morning.

"How would you like to see a vendue, Jenny?"

Scrunching her nose, Jenny shrugged her shoulders and asked, "What's that?"

"A vendue is a public auction," Papa explained. "Poor people are auctioned off to the lowest bidders."

"Lowest bidders? Don't you mean highest?"

"No. At a vendue people from the poorhouse go to the bidder who offers food and lodging at the lowest price. The settlement pays for them to be cared for. Then the poor work on the farms or in the houses where they are kept."

"You mean the settlement is selling people for work? Isn't that like slavery, Papa? That's really bad. Mamma even said it was really bad."

"Well, it isn't too different from slavery except these people need help. The community can't afford to keep them very long and if the people don't find someone to help them, they might starve or freeze to death in winter."

"Papa, that's horrible."

Just then a horn blew in the town square. People from all around began to gather. Papa nudged Jenny forward. She knew Mamma would not like the idea of her going to a vendue, but here they were.

Stooping down Papa whispered in a serious tone, "Don't go telling your mother about this."

Jenny nodded, and she and Papa stood at the edge of the crowd.

An auctioneer pointed his stick at an old woman, instructing her to stand tall. "Old beggar widow," he said loudly. "This poor woman could be your own mother. She's alone and starving. Do I have a bid for her keep?"

When no one offered a bid, the auctioneer told a terrible story about the woman that made everyone feel sad and uncomfortable for her. One woman in the audience bid a very low price and was allowed to take possession of her. A representative from the settlement gave the woman some coins and she left with the old widow.

Next an old man who could hardly stand was brought to the front. "Open your mouth," demanded the auctioneer. The sad old man opened his mouth and showed a gaping hole with only a few teeth, most of them broken.

"Look. No teeth. This one will be easy to feed. He'll live well on **gruel**," called the auctioneer. A few people made bids, mostly out of mercy, and the old man was led away.

Next came a young woman dressed in rags. Shaking, she presented herself before the crowd. With pride she said, "I can clean and cook. I'm strong." Many people offered bids for the young woman and she was soon led away in tears. The man who bid the lowest was the canal superintendent that Papa had argued with the night before.

By this time Papa felt so bad for these people he could stand it no longer. "Let's be moving on," he said in a sad tone, and they pushed a path through the crowd.

Just then the auctioneer cleared his throat and a whisper went through the crowd. "Ladies and gentlemen, don't let the color of this boy's hair raise a fear in your hearts. He's an untarnished **urchin** from the swamps."

Turning quickly, both Jenny and Papa saw the red-haired boy standing straight and steady, glaring out at the audience.

"He's thin, but he can be fattened up. Ladies, please don't be afraid. This is 1836, and there is no place for superstitions. The boy's a foundling left by the epidemic to fend for himself. Have we bids to take this boy?"

One man raised his hand, but his wife quickly pulled it down saying, "We don't want no witching boy on our farm!"

"Can ya read, boy?" asked the auctioneer. The boy shook his head. "Well now, neither can a lot of folks. See, no learning to set this boy above his keepers.

"Ya got to smile, boy. Don't you want to go home with some of these nice folks?"

"No!" shouted the boy. The auctioneer clunked him on the side of the head with his long stick.

"Papa, do something. This is awful!" cried Jenny.

"Now what's the offer for this urchin?" called the dealer, putting an iron grip on the boy's shoulder.

"I'll keep him for a **king's ransom**," called a man in a tall black hat. The people around him laughed and agreed.

In an effort to break away, the boy knocked the auctioneer off balance. Cursing and swinging wildly, the auctioneer was unable to regain his strong grasp on his prisoner. The boy pushed through the crowd, scrambling his way to freedom.

An old man reached out with a cane and tripped the boy. Another man grabbed his arm and dragged him back to the auctioneer. Some of the crowd cheered.

"Papa. . .," began Jenny.

"I'll take the boy," shouted Papa, and the crowd quieted almost instantly. "And I don't want a penny of the settlement's money."

"My good sir," responded the auctioneer. "That is not how it works."

"I'll take him, blast you all!" cried Papa. "A human life isn't something to be sold."

"What kind of talk is this?" howled the auctioneer. "You forget yourself, sir."

"No, you people have forgotten yourselves. Where is your charity? Your goodness of heart? Why are we better than these poor people who have stood here in this square today? I'll take the boy."

The crowd parted and let Papa pass. He reached out and took the boy by the arm, escorting him as if he were a prince. No one spoke as Papa passed by with dignity.

Jenny ran to catch up. She was so proud she thought her heart would burst. Papa was a good man. But what would Mamma say?

As the three made their way back to the boat, they could see the *William and Mary* being loaded with freight. Papa boarded with the boy and went directly below without a word to Uncle McKee. Jenny decided to remain safely on deck.

Soon Aunt Emma hurried up the stairs. Jenny heard her father's stern voice, but very little from Mamma. Then Papa came up, pulled his pipe from his vest pocket, and began to puff away.

Mamma stomped up the stairs and announced, "You might have brought me a boy, but he is not my son. And he'll be scrubbed before he is allowed into this cabin to stay!"

Mamma stomped back down the steps and soon Jenny heard a great rattling of pans. Aunt Emma brought down a big wash tub and quickly returned to the deck.

"You've done it now, Richard Case," she said as she passed Papa. Papa just puffed his pipe with a stern look on his face.

"The boy is welcome here, Case," said Uncle McKee as he approached Papa. "But until we know his sort, I prefer he sleeps on the deck."

Papa nodded silently and stared up the canal as McKee directed the hoggee to get the boat underway. Jenny understood his sadness for the people they had seen auctioned that morning. She walked up beside him and slipped her hand into his. She was proud to be his daughter.

The afternoon passed quickly and by supper Mamma had scrubbed the boy so clean his skin shone a bright pink. He wore a pair of Papa's pants rolled up in bunches around his knees and his shirt was an old flour sack that Aunt Emma had cut armholes in. He was a sight, and Jenny could hardly keep from giggling.

At supper the boy ate as if he had never had a real meal in his life. He slurped and gobbled and burped, and then started all over again. When he finally slowed down Uncle McKee asked, "How old are ya, boy?"

"Dunno," he returned with a defiant look.

"For all the stars in heaven, boy, make a guess!" said Uncle.

The boy shrugged, rolled up a piece of bread and stuffed it into his mouth.

"That will be enough of that!" instructed Mamma. "It's sad you've had no proper home, but now you have one, you'll not be acting like an animal at my table."

The boy tried to quickly swallow the ball of bread and choked. Panicking, he coughed hard. The bread flew out of his mouth and onto the table.

"It's a fine bit of goods ya got there, Mr. Case," growled Uncle McKee as he abruptly left the table. Aunt Emma followed him with his mug of coffee.

Glaring at Papa, Mamma wiped the table. Jenny, afraid of what would happen next, decided to break the silence. "What's your name?" she asked the boy.

He shrugged, looking downward. "Ain't got any."

"Surely, you have to have a name," Mamma insisted.

"None. Everyone just calls me boy or witchy boy or wild carrot."

"The boy has got to have a proper name, Richard. This just won't do."

"Call him after me," said Papa. "Give him my name. It's what Jenny was going to be called before she was born a girl. So give him my name."

The boy looked up and stared at Papa. Mamma, even more surprised, swallowed hard. "Richard? Well, husband, if that's what you want, then that is what it will be—Richard."

Upset again, Mamma cleared the table of dishes and started washing them in a noisy manner. If she had only seen the vendue, thought Jenny, she would have known why Papa had brought the boy into the family.

"Where's your folks, son—Richard," Papa asked.

The boy shook his head. "Ain't got any."

"The boy's a foundling, Mother. He has no folks." Mamma ignored Papa and continued with the dishes.

After dinner Papa took blankets from the trunk and made a bed for Richard on the deck. With a full stomach and clean, warm blankets, the boy soon fell asleep.

The rest of the evening Mamma remained silent, even refusing to talk with Aunt Emma. When Jenny went to bed early, Mamma followed. She took the center cot and soon fell into a **fitful** sleep.

Jenny lay awake, wondering about the boy. Was he now her brother, or would he be gone in the morning, a runaway? And where was his dog?

Chapter 5
Making Friends

The next morning Jenny rose early and dressed quietly. Making her way to the deck, she found the boy among the boxes, rolled up in his blanket. A brown nose poked out from under the blanket. Two eyes glared up at her, one brown and the other blue. It was the dog.

As she came closer, the dog slipped from under the covers. It faced Jenny and growled, showing its long fangs.

Throwing the covers from his head, the boy quickly sat up. "It's just you. What do ya want?" he asked as he blinked the sleep from his eyes.

"I won't tell, but if Uncle McKee catches the dog here he might shoot it. He thinks it's a wolf."

The boy patted his dog. "She ain't no wolf. Ya can tell by the different color eyes. She ain't no wolf. That's crazy."

"Don't you remember when Uncle tried to shoot her? I pushed him so his gun would miss. I like wolves or wolf-dogs."

"I thought he was just being mean to me. Bait me in with food and shoot for the fun of it. People do it, ya know."

Just then they heard Uncle McKee's voice below. Hopping to his feet, the boy pushed the dog to the side of the boat where it leaped to the bank and ran to the woods.

Not far down the trail Jenny spotted the hoggee with his team. Stopping dead in their tracks, the team pulled back and stomped their feet.

With a mug of coffee in his hand, Uncle McKee came up the stairs to the deck. He frowned when he saw Jenny and the boy. "What are you two up to?"

Just then the three on deck heard the hoggee **cussing** at his team,

"What's the matter?"

"Don't know, McKee," shouted the hoggee. "Something in the woods is spooking 'em." Struggling with the team, he soon managed to hitch them to the towline. Uncle McKee took the tiller and the *William and Mary* moved to the center of the canal.

Unsure how to make friends with the boy, Jenny asked, "Did you really live in the swamps with a witch?"

Anger spread over the boy's face. "She weren't no witch, just an old African woman. She escaped from the Carolinas. Came to New York State on the Underground Railroad."

Wide-eyed Jenny asked, "What's that?"

"Don't you know nothin'? It's secret safe places for slaves to hide if they're running away north. It can be a house or barn or shed. Just that it's owned by someone who wants to help slaves get away. These places are sorta like a train that moves people from slavery to freedom. Only it's the slaves that do the movin'."

Jenny was surprised. She had heard about slaves and runaways, but never about the Underground Railroad.

"The old woman was born into slavery. Her owners were mean. She had babies and they took 'em away. Sold 'em." The boy pushed his face up close to Jenny's, "So don't be calling her a witch anymore, ya hear?"

"I wasn't meaning any disrespect. Really. I just heard it said. Where's the old woman now?"

"Up yonder," he said, pointing at the sky.

"She's dead?"

"Yep. She's gone. The **influenza** got her in the spring. She'd be old now anyhow. She was all of fifty summers. She always said, 'Life is good if ya don't weaken.' I guess she meant that if ya weaken it's too hard to live.

"She taught me what she knew, specially all her learning 'bout plants. I know a plant that takes the poison from a snake bite. And one that cools fevers. I know plants that make you dead as a corpse. In an instant."

Jenny's eyes widened. "I don't believe you. I've lived on a farm all my life and I never knew plants that could do those things."

"Wild plants. Farmers don't know nothing 'bout wild plants. Indians do. Indians showed the old woman.

"You're a puny little girl. I'll bet you're afraid of Indians. I'm not. They're my friends. Brought food and medicine to the old woman and me when we had needs."

Jenny interrupted, "I'm not afraid of Indians. I had my own Indian friend. He used to bring me berries and he brought fish and meat to Mamma."

For the first time the boy smiled. "There aren't many that trust people like Africans or Indians.

Guess 'cause they're different in their ways and seem scary."

"Most are just misunderstood," said Jenny, repeating what Papa had always said.

The boy smiled again. "Guess if you folks believe that, I can stay around for awhile, too. At least until I go west. I want to meet some more Indians and hunt those big critters called buffalo."

"We're going west, but not that far. You're going to go with us. Papa even said," exclaimed Jenny. "We're going to the Territory of Michigan on the other side of Lake Erie. First we get to ride on a big steamboat to Toledo. Then we'll buy a wagon and go to the Territory."

"Well, I got some plans, but maybe I'll stay with you awhile, 'specially if this Territory is really west," answered the boy.

"It's west, all right. All the way across Lake Erie."

"Is that a big lake?"

"It's really big. On the other side, there is even another country—Canada. At one end it has those big falls called Niagara."

The boy scrunched up his freckled nose in disbelief.

"You mean you never read about those falls between Lake Erie and Lake Ontario?"

The boy shrugged. "I don't know how to read. I heard talk of books, but I ain't never seen one."

Jenny couldn't believe what she was hearing. Quickly she dashed below, threw open the lid to the trunk, and began digging through it.

Hearing the commotion, Mamma came into the cabin. "What are you doing, young lady. Stop pawing through our things like that."

"Mamma, that boy can't read. He never even saw a book before. I want to show him one of ours."

"Here, let me," said Mamma. Carefully she reached deep into the trunk and brought out two books. "In my opinion, there aren't two better books in the world to learn from." She handed Jenny a large black Bible and another book that the man gave to Papa with their land deed. Its title read, *John Mason Peck: A New Guide for Emigrants to the West, Containing Sketches of Ohio, Indiana, Illinois, Missouri, and Michigan with the Territories of Wisconsin and Arkansas, and the Adjacent Parts.*

"Isn't that the longest title you've ever heard?" asked Mamma. "But I've been looking through it, and it's mighty interesting."

Jenny grabbed the books and ran to the stairs.

"Walk. A lady walks. She doesn't run," reminded Mamma.

Jenny stopped, holding herself back in her excitement.

"Don't forget I packed your slate, too. You need work on your writing. And I hope you're keeping up on your journal."

"Yes, Mamma," said Jenny as she slowly made her way to the deck in a manner fitting a proper lady.

Standing by the open trunk, Mamma smiled and remembered her years as a teacher and how excited she had been to teach others to read.

On deck, Jenny placed the books on the supply boxes and opened them. Richard ran his hands over the pages as he turned them one at a time. "All these squiggles mean something?"

"Yes. The squiggles are letters and they are all part of the alphabet. This book has maps, too," she said as she turned the pages of the *New Guide for Emigrants*. "This is Lake Erie. And here are the great falls at Niagara."

Turning the page she found a map of the mitten territory. Here's where we're going. First to Buffalo, then to Toledo, and then the Territory." Jenny touched each location with her finger.

"Which way is west?" asked Richard.

Jenny showed him the compass rose at the bottom of the page. "Up is north and down is south. Right is east and left is west. You do know left and right, don't you?" asked Jenny.

"Gee and haw. That's right and left—gee and haw."

Jenny frowned.

"You ain't so smart if ya don't know gee and haw is right and left. Mules and horses on the path know that. Ya say 'gee' to make 'em go right and 'haw' to make them go left."

Jenny scratched her head.

"Betcha I can read something you can't. I can read the weather. The old woman taught me that. When the leaves blow upside down and show silver color underneath, it's gonna rain. When clouds get low and heavy and the wind picks up and you can smell the rain, you know it's on the way.

"In fact, if things keep going as they are, we'll have rain before noon. I can smell it. Readin' the sky, though, is easier than readin' squiggles," said the boy.

Jenny looked around and noticed the wind had begun to blow gently. Along the canal the leaves on the trees were beginning to show their bottoms. "I better tell Uncle. I'm going to get my slate, too, so you can learn your squiggles."

As Jenny passed Uncle McKee she suggested, "You better get **oilcloths** out for the freight because Richard said it's going to rain. He knows about reading the weather. He said he thinks it will rain before center sun."

"He reads weather?" questioned McKee. "Well, you tell him to just keep readin' away because I'm captain of this boat. You tell that boy that I'm the only one that decides when to pull out the oilcloths. You tell that boy. . .."

"Richard, his name is Richard," interrupted Jenny. "He's called after Papa now."

"You tell that boy he's to be mindin' his own business and I'll be mindin' the business of the canal," Uncle McKee stared down at Jenny.

Surprised by his response, Jenny went slowly below. As she returned with her slate and chalk, she noticed that the leaves were starting to look silver.

"Uncle McKee doesn't want any advice. He said he'd take care of his canal business and it was none of yours."

Richard shrugged.

"You want to learn your letters now?" asked Jenny. Sitting on a box beside Richard she wrote the alphabet in her best handwriting. "Now, you try to copy them."

Richard gripped the chalk tightly. Pressing hard, he snapped off the end.

"Not so hard, Richard."

He tried again, this time clumsily copying the letter A. "This ain't so hard. Bet I can learn to read today."

Jenny laughed. "It takes time. I was six when I started. Now I'm eleven and still learning words."

"Well, that's because you're a girl. Girls take longer to learn."

"They do not," said Jenny hotly. "Girls are just as smart as boys, even smarter."

Richard grinned.

With one hand Jenny shoved Richard back over the box he was sitting on. "Don't be making fun of me, Richard. You're just a stupid old boy. Now pick yourself up and write your alphabet," she demanded.

Richard laughed. "You're pretty perky, for a girl."

Jenny stomped her foot and handed the chalk and slate back to Richard. Again he made a letter.

"That's the letter 'B.' If you were smart, you'd know that."

Richard looked up with a grin. "You mean if I was smart like a gal?"

"That's right. Smart like a girl."

Richard made the letter 'C.'

"If you were smart as a girl," taunted Jenny, "you wouldn't be so sloppy and clumsy with your letters."

"I ain't clumsy. My letters look like yours."

"They do not."

"They do so," shouted Richard as he stood facing Jenny.

"They do not," cried Jenny as she gave Richard a push.

"They do so!" said Richard as he pushed back with all his might. This time Jenny fell backwards, losing her balance and toppling over the side of the boat into the dirty water of the canal.

Jenny hit the water with a huge splash, sinking downward. She tried to struggle to the surface, but her long skirt and apron twisted around her. Then, in an instant, she felt something beside her, nudging her to the surface.

As she broke water, Jenny gasped for air. She reached for the boat, and realized the dog was beside her, her sleeve in its mouth. By the time Aunt Emma, Uncle McKee, Mamma, and Papa ran to her rescue, the dog had disappeared around the side of the boat.

"Jenny, are you all right?" called Papa.

"Yes," she said as she reached for his extended hand.

"Landsakes, daughter, do I have to chain you to the boat so I can hear the rattling if you fall overboard?" he joked. With both hands he pulled Jenny from the dirty canal.

"Fall in? The girl didn't fall in. This here boy shoved her in." Uncle McKee held Richard roughly by the back of the neck and began to shake him.

"McKee, leave the boy be," insisted Papa.

McKee gave Richard a shove, knocking him to the deck.

"Jenny, is that true? Did the boy push you in?" demanded Mamma.

"The boy's name is Richard, Mamma, and no, he didn't push me in."

"Don't be sassy to your mother," said Papa. "I want the truth."

"Well, his name is Richard and he didn't push me in. We were just playing. I pushed him first."

"See, I told you there would be trouble," said Mamma. "Now it's already started." She pulled Jenny by the arm and directed her below.

"Don't be talking that way to me, wife. The children were just playing."

"Playin' indeed," interrupted Uncle McKee. "I saw it, Case. The boy pushed her."

Pulling away from Mamma Jenny hollered, "His name is Richard! Richard! His name is Richard!"

"Jenny! Mind your elders and don't be raising your voice to Uncle," demanded Mamma.

"Oh, my!" said Aunt Emma as she gazed away from the argument. "Isn't it a beauty?"

Everyone's attention turned to Richard who was pulling the dog from the canal.

"A beauty, woman? What's wrong with your head? It's the dang wolf. Get me my gun!"

Richard ran toward Uncle McKee to stop him. "It ain't a wolf! It ain't a wolf! Can't you see it ain't a wolf?" he shouted as Uncle McKee pushed him away.

To protect the dog, Jenny ran and wrapped her arms around the animal's neck. "She saved me when I fell into the canal. She kept me from drowning."

"Jenny, no!" cried Mamma. "Get away from that animal."

"Jenny, girl, move away slow," instructed McKee. The dog made a low growl and showed her teeth at McKee.

"Jenny, be careful. Come to your uncle. The wolf won't hurt you if you move slow."

"It ain't a wolf," insisted Richard. "Look at her eyes."

"Yes," agreed Aunt Emma. "I've never seen eyes like those on a wolf."

"That's true," said Mamma. "Wolves wouldn't have two different colored eyes, would they husband?"

"By gol," said Papa. "If that isn't the darndest thing. It does have two different colored eyes. The children are right, McKee. This is no wolf."

"If it ain't a wolf, why does it look like a wolf and growl and show its teeth like one?"

"Well, when you act like an animal yourself, husband," said Emma, "I'd like to growl and show my teeth at you, too."

"Now don't be talkin' to me that way, woman." Uncle McKee turned in time to see an angry, look cross Aunt Emma's face.

"That will be the end of it," insisted Emma. "This isn't a wolf, it's a dog. Maybe a wolf-dog, but it's the boy's pet. That's all there is to it."

"A dog? A pet? There are no pets on the canal."

"There are plenty of pets on the canal," retorted Aunt Emma. "Why, there are lots of cats."

"That's to take care of rats and mice in the grain."

"What about those green birds?"

"What?"

"Those green birds that the captain of the *Whirlwind* has. The birds that repeat all those bad cuss words."

"Those are South American parrots," said Uncle McKee. "They're rare."

"Well, they're pets, aren't they?"

Uncle stood for a minute with a blank expression. "Oh, for the love of Mike!" he said stomping away.

Jenny stood and let go of the dog who now wagged her tail and sat calmly.

Aunt Emma, not finished with the discussion, followed Uncle McKee. Standing with her hands on her hips and facing Uncle squarely she said, "Is this the way you'll treat our son if he wants a pet?"

McKee cocked his head with a questioning look on his face and then began to grin. "What are you sayin', wife? Are we gonna be havin' a wee one?"

The look on Uncle McKee's face made everyone smile. He picked Aunt Emma up, swinging her high in the air and forgetting the exchange that had just passed between them.

Aunt Emma squealed with delight.

"Oh, did I hurt ya, darling?" he asked as he gently put her on her feet.

Just then a rumble of thunder echoed down the canal. "We told you it was going to rain," scolded Jenny. "Richard said it was going to rain and you didn't believe him."

"Jenny, behave yourself," interrupted Mamma. "You've caused enough trouble today. I want you to go below and change before you catch your death."

McKee and Papa scrambled for the oilcloths that were packed below, and soon all the freight was covered with the waterproof cloths. Pulling on his **oil-skin** poncho, Uncle McKee returned to the tiller as the sky opened and the rain began to beat on the boat.

Below Jenny changed into dry clothes and sat with Richard on the kitchen steps. "Maybe Uncle will just forget about us and the dog," Jenny whispered.

Just then Uncle McKee called down the stairs to Richard. "I won't be shootin' that wolf of yours, boy. But I don't want it aboard the *William and Mary*, you hear me? Animals have fleas and carry diseases. I won't be takin' no chances.

"As soon as the rain stops, I want it off. It can follow along the path as long as it doesn't bother the hoggee and team. And you ain't to be feedin' it our food. It'll have to fend for itself in the woods."

Aunt Emma peeked up the stairs and interrupted, "Well, since the superintendent won't be welcome to supper anymore, there will be plenty of unclaimed scraps the dog can eat."

"Wife, you ain't helping matters!" returned the exasperated McKee.

Emma smiled and winked at Jenny and Richard.

In the afternoon the weather cleared and the sun shone brightly, as if the sky had been washed clean by the rain. McKee pulled the boat to the bank and Jenny, Richard, and the dog hopped off. Mamma and

Papa watched as the three ran and played together along the path. "That girl is wild already and we haven't even reached the wilderness," said Mamma.

Papa just smiled. "She'll be fine, especially now that she has a brother and dog to keep her company."

"She might have a brother and dog, but she hasn't got a wearable sunbonnet," Mamma complained. "I found her bonnet in the boy's shirt when I scrubbed him down, but there was sausage and bread in it."

Papa smiled. "Just boil it with his clothes."

Mamma shook her head and smiled, slipping her hand around Papa's arm. "Maybe it's time to boil some settlement water and set a line."

Chapter 6
New Adventures

The next morning Jenny pulled her pink-flowered sunbonnet from the wash line and tied it around her neck. Richard stretched in the sunlight in his clean, old clothes. "I don't remember these clothes being boiled before. I think I like them this way. Your ma says it kills the bugs."

From under her apron Jenny pulled a cloth with a sausage and a half-eaten piece of bread in it. "It's for the dog. But we can't let Uncle catch us throwing it to her, so I have an idea." She whispered into Richard's ear.

Richard smiled and nodded. Putting his fingers to his lips, he whistled shrilly. Seconds later the dog came bounding from the underbrush to the path.

"Ya want off?" called Uncle McKee.

"Yes please," Jenny responded.

Uncle directed the boat to the bank. As it drew near, Jenny reached over and gave him a soft kiss on the cheek. Surprised and flattered, McKee smiled. "Thank you, missy."

By that time Richard had tossed the dog's food into the woods, and the dog disappeared to eat it.

Noticing the dog's disappearance, Uncle commented, "Looks like she don't want your company today," he laughed. "Maybe soon she'll forget you and stop following the boat."

"You're probably right, Uncle," smiled Jenny sweetly. "Maybe we should just stay on board so Richard can work on his alphabet."

Jenny quickly got her slate and books and the two sat on the low pitch of the cabin roof. "Where'd you say we are going?" inquired Richard as he picked up the book with maps.

"To the Territory of Michigan."

"No, you said somewhere before that."

"Buffalo?"

Richard shook his head.

"To Toledo?"

"That's it. I heard people in the settlement talking about that place. I heard it said there's a war going on there."

"A war? There's no war going on in the United States," insisted Jenny.

"Well, that's what they said. The people in Michigan want their terrritory to be a state. They say Toledo should be in it, but Toledo is already part of another state."

"Maybe it's part of Ohio. That's close by," said Jenny. "Let's look at the map." Turning to the page of the mitten territory Jenny could see Toledo at a bend along Lake Erie. "The map says it's in Michigan."

"Well, I heard Ohio wants it. And the folks of the territory say its theirs. That's why there's a war."

Jenny wasn't sure if she believed Richard. She wondered if Papa knew anything about a war.

"Well, as I see it," said Richard, "if there's a war we should go on farther west. We could go far enough to live with Indians and hunt buffaloes."

Overhearing their conversation, Uncle McKee interrupted. "Boy, ya don't know what you're talking about. I ain't heard nothing about no war. So stop scaring the girl."

"He knew when it was going to rain," snapped Jenny. "You didn't know that either."

"Don't be sassy with me, miss. Why don't you go below and work with the women. You need to learn your place."

Jenny grabbed the books and slate and stormed below. She knew her place, she thought, she was a teacher.

It was shortly after supper that thunder again began to rumble along the canal. Bright flashes of lightning lit the sky and once again there was a steady downpour of rain.

All evening the rain continued. Jenny lay awake on her cot long after Mamma had come to bed. She drifted in and out of sleep as the rain slapped the roof of the *William and Mary*.

Suddenly, she heard something strange outside. There were voices of men along the canal. Quietly, Jenny rolled from her cot and crept up the stairs. Looking up the canal she could see nothing in the dark night. But just then a strange looking boat appeared behind the *William and Mary*. A hoggee dressed in an oilskin poncho pulled his team past Uncle's McKee's boat.

Just then Richard came out of the darkness and stopped short when he saw Jenny. "What are you doing out here?" he said with a start. "Get inside. This is none of your business."

"What's going on? What are you doing?" demanded Jenny.

"It's a 'hurry-up' boat. There's a hole in the **berm.** They'll give me coins if I help. Where's your uncle's oilskin?" he asked, feeling around under the oilcloths that covered the freight. "I'll be back in the morning as soon as the job is done."

"I want to go," pleaded Jenny.

"You can't, you're a girl. Tell 'em I'll be back in the morning." Without finding the poncho Richard turned and ran to the back of the boat, jumping from the *William and Mary* and onto the "hurry-up" boat.

Jenny was now wide awake and wished with all her might that she were a boy and could go make money repairing a hole. Starting down the steps to the cabin, she reached out her hand to find the way. There, along the wall, she felt Uncle McKee's oilskin poncho.

Grabbing the poncho from its nail, Jenny darted back up the steps just as the stern of the "hurry-up" boat passed the bow of the *William and Mary.* In an instant she leaped onto the work boat. As she landed barefoot, she slipped and fell on the wet, muddy deck.

At first Jenny wanted to cry, but she knew she would be discovered. Biting her lip she stood up in the rain, afraid she had made a mistake. She slipped her uncle's poncho over her head. It was so big she felt nearly lost in it.

Near the front of the boat Jenny could see lanterns and shadows of men in oilskins. As she edged her way along the deck, she realized the boat was quite different from the *William and Mary*. Instead of a large cabin there was an open deck with piles of dirt, shovels, boards, and other equipment.

"Well, fellas—what have we here?" came a booming voice behind Jenny.

Startled, Jenny turned quickly and stared into the face of a wrinkled old man.

"I'm here. . .I'm here to earn some coins mending the hole," she blurted out bravely.

The old man laughed. "You better come on up here with the rest of the crew so we can get a look at you."

Jenny followed the man and soon recognized Richard, standing with the others. He now wore an old oilskin.

"What in tar-nation are ya doin' here?" he yelled. "Your folks will think I've gone and kidnapped ya."

"You know her, Carrot?" asked the old man.

"I know her. She belongs with those folks goin' to the Michigan Territory. You're a dumb girl," he cried as he turned his attention back to Jenny.

Jenny hung her head and felt like she was going to cry.

"Here now," said the old man. "We can use all the help we can get. There'll be other women folk helping. I heard they were waking all the farms. There'll be work for us all."

Jenny looked up and the rain washed away her tears before anyone could notice. "I only wanted to help."

Richard shook his head and walked away as the men all laughed. "Women are mighty stubborn when they want to do something, boy. You best get used to it now," said one of them.

Jenny followed Richard. "I'm sorry I came."

"I'm sorry you came, too," said Richard with a scowl.

"I was just going to bring you Uncle McKee's poncho, but then I thought I could help, too."

"You'll be in the way. You're just a girl."

"They said other women would be helping."

"They're different. They live by the canal and know what to do and how to stay outta men's way."

"You tell me what to do, and I'll do it. I can learn."

"Go back to the *William and Mary*, then, before you're missed."

Jenny crossed her arms under her poncho and turned from Richard. "What's all that dirt for?"

"To fill the hole."

"What's all the lumber for?"

"To fill the hole. Don't ya know nothing? This here's a "hurry-up" boat. There's one every thirty miles along the canal. They keep the canal repaired. If a hole ain't repaired, it will flood all the farms around here for miles and drain all the water out of the canal, too.

"When ya got water where it don't belong, ya got mad farmers. And when ya got boats stuck on the bottom, ya got mad captains. And I don't want to be around when that happens.

"Look, those are farmers coming to help," pointed Richard. Jenny looked up and saw lights coming across a field. As the boat rounded a curve in the canal, she saw dozens of people with flickering lanterns working along the muddy bank.

"It's the biggest mess I've ever seen," yelled one man from the bank.

As the "hurry-up" boat pulled to the bank, the men began jumping off. The old man quickly gave Jenny the job of handing lanterns, wooden mallets, and shovels to men along the bank. When she finished, she carefully hopped to the bank.

"The water level's dropping," shouted a man.

"We need three feet! Do we still have three feet?" called the old man from the boat. "Them boats won't float—none of them—without three feet of water."

A man standing chest deep in water called, "It's here now, but not for long if we don't get this hole plugged."

"The bank is washin' away faster than we can fill it," someone yelled.

Men splashed into the canal carrying wooden mallets. Long planks were handed down to them. With heavy plunk, plunk, plunks the men drove the plank **pilings** deep into the canal with their mallets.

As Jenny grew accustomed to the darkness she could see Richard standing at the hole's edge handing the men tools and holding a lantern. Nearby there were women pulling in brush and hay to fill the hole. She ran to help them as they struggled in the mud.

Soon people arrived with a wagon full of dry wood. They started a huge bonfire that helped light the night for the workers. The weary men who had been driving in the pilings pulled themselves from the water and were replaced by a group of fresh workers.

Jenny could see that the hole was getting bigger. Mud and dirt broke away. The water was biting into the land and even taking away parts of the towpath. Excitement and fear could now be seen in everyone's faces.

Teams of horses pulled huge logs to the canal's edge. Workers rolled the first log down the bank. It splashed into the water, twisting and twirling with the current. With great urgency and strength the men in the canal struggled to lodge the log against the pilings. Then workers rolled another log off the bank. Jenny could see what they were trying to do. They were making a wall of logs to rebuild the bank, plugging the hole.

"Is it gonna hold?" called a man.

"I don't know, the water's pourin' through it."

"We can't lose her. . .. Get another log. We need something to slow the water."

Richard worked with a team of horses to tow more logs to the breach. With the other women and children, Jenny dumped branches and brush into the hole. But the water was moving so fast it washed most of it away.

Jenny wished there was more she could do. If only there was something to cover the gaps between the logs long enough to slow the water, she thought, the brush and hay would stay in place and they could fill the hole.

Thinking for a moment, she quickly pulled off her large poncho. Maybe this will work, she thought. Standing at the edge of the hole she tossed her poncho, open like a big cape, against the pilings. The swirling current pulled it beneath the water. Then the poncho caught on the brush and was sucked hard against the wall.

The water started to slow. In an instant the men started shedding their oilskins, tossing them against the pilings. Women piled in more brush, then hay. Soon the men were able to start shoveling dirt in the hole.

"It's working! It's working!" called the old man from the "hurry-up" boat.

Exhausted, wet, and cold, Jenny stood watching as the current slowed and the hole was slowly filled. "That was right smart thinking for a girl," said an old woman as she passed Jenny.

Soon another woman came to Jenny, covering her shoulders with a blanket. "You saved our farm tonight, miss. Come by the fire and warm yourself."

Jenny moved toward the fire and sat down on the wet, cold ground. As she pulled the blanket up around her she felt a nudge. Looking up, Jenny saw the two-colored eyes of her friend. She opened the blanket and the dog joined her. Together they shared each other's warmth as the dog licked Jenny's face. Giggling, Jenny rested her head against the dog and quickly fell asleep.

The next thing Jenny knew she was being handed over into Papa's arms aboard the *William and Mary*. Waking with a start she heard her mother's voice. "What did you do to her?" she cried to Richard. "Where's she been?" Mamma grabbed Richard by the ear and shook him. Richard, covered with mud, howled and tried to pull away.

"That boy is trouble. I said it all along," cried Mamma. "Now look at our girl."

"It wasn't his fault," said Jenny softly. "I went because I wanted to."

The old man from the "hurry-up" boat stepped over onto the *William and Mary*. "I think I better explain what's been happening tonight, ma'am."

The old man waved the "hurry-up" boat on, and Aunt Emma, who had already made coffee, lit another lantern in the kitchen. Uncle McKee poured mugs of coffee and Aunt Emma took Richard into her cabin to find dry clothes for him to wear.

Mamma, madder than ever before, led Jenny by the arm into the women's cabin. She pulled out towels and dry clothes from the trunk. "Don't be saying a word 'til I find out the facts," she said shaking her finger at Jenny. Pushing past the curtain she returned to the kitchen.

After Jenny dried and changed her clothes, she joined the group. Richard sat on the floor by the stove, dressed in a pair of Uncle McKee's pants and one of his shirts. He hung his head, nearly asleep in the kitchen's warmth.

As the grown-ups sipped coffee, the old man told them the story about the hole in the canal and how Jenny's quick thinking helped to save the valley. Papa reached over and rubbed Jenny's shoulder. "You nearly scared us all to death when we found you missing. We didn't know what to think."

"I'm sorry," said Jenny, looking up at Papa. "It wasn't Richard's fault. He didn't even know I followed him. He was just going to earn some coins, and I just wanted to help."

"Do ya own a wolf-dog?" the old man interrupted.

"Why do ya ask?" questioned McKee.

"Oh, nothing. . .just saw the darndest thing. When we were about to leave we spied the girl all cuddled up with this big animal.

"At first we thought it was a wolf. It sat right next to the girl, growling and showing its teeth."

Uncle McKee looked at Papa and shook his head.

"But when we got a look at those two-colored eyes, we figured it was some sort of dog, or at least part dog."

"You say it was keeping Jenny warm?" asked Mamma.

"Protecting her, too. It wouldn't let none of us near her. We were about to poke the girl with a stick when the boy came along. He woke the girl up long enough to get her to the boat, and the critter just took to the woods.

"I just wanted to let you know. 'Cause if it was yours, we didn't bring it back with us."

Aunt Emma smiled with satisfaction, while Uncle McKee quickly decided to change the subject. "Old man," asked Uncle, "have you heard anything about trouble in the Michigan Territory?"

"You meaning the war?"

"The Toledo War, that's the one," interrupted Richard who was now wide awake.

"I've heard nothing about this," said Papa. "What's it all about?"

"The way it was told to me, there's a wedge of land running maybe five miles wide in Indiana to about eight wide in O-hi. This wedge is what's causing the problem. Making a land war.

"Young Mason, the acting governor, thought it was time for the territory to be a state. Well, when he was working on it he discovered O-hi had been claiming Port Lawrence and Vistula. That's what we call Toledo.

"Lucas, governor of O-hi, signed an act claiming his state's border ran from the southern point of Lake Michigan to the north shore of Maumee Bay. That gave O-hi possession of the harbor along the Erie.

"Mason, not liking the act, let his temper rise. They say he is red-haired, like your boy here."

Richard smiled, happy to hear that someone with red hair was so important in the Michigan Territory.

"That man, being a **hotspur**, went right to address President Andrew Jackson about the matter. At first Jackson sided with the Territory. But Lucas, a friend of the President, came forward. He claimed that his people tolerated the chicken thieving that had gone on for years from the Territory. But now the Territory people wanted to steal lands and that was a different matter. He would not stand for it.

"Lucas swayed the President, which angered Mason. It's also said Lucas called Mason a 'most savage person,' and the fight was on."

Mamma, taking Papa's hand, cast a frightened look across the table to the old man.

"There's nothing to be frightened of, ma'am. This has been going on now for some time. Awhile back Mason got up a militia and went to the border. He arrested some surveyors trying to set down the Ohio line. Then O-hi got up a militia. Lucas said about ten thousand would show, but only a few hundred volunteers came. I guess the people of O-hi weren't as concerned as Lucas.

"Now there's lots more to the story, but I don't recall it offhand."

"Is it over?" asked Papa anxiously. "Did it get settled? Will Michigan be a state?"

"Well, I heard along the canal that the Territory's set in motion to become a state. But the uproar over that Toledo Strip, as they call it, is still going on along the border."

"Has anyone been hurt?" asked Mamma.

"Just their pride. I do believe a couple of horses or mules were shot by accident. There were reports of chickens and pigs being stolen from border farms. But that ain't nothing new.

"I wouldn't be too concerned. If the Territory is where you're heading, it'll be a state in a few months. But if I were going to the Territory by way of Toledo, I might reconsider. Not that there would probably be any danger, but you never can tell what you'll run into."

Papa, satisfied with what he heard nodded in agreement. "We thank you for the information."

Standing, the old man opened a small bag that was attached to a chain around his neck. He tossed a couple of shiny coins onto the table. "This here is the money for the children's work."

Jenny looked at Richard with a wide grin on her face. Mamma reached out and picked up the money, putting the coins in her pocket.

Chapter 7
Montezuma Medicine

The next morning Jenny slept late and the hoggee and team were already at work before she came on deck. Uncle McKee was at the tiller, and he quickly told her to remain quiet today because Papa wasn't feeling well.

Rushing down to the kitchen, Jenny found Mamma boiling water and looking very tired. "Jenny, your father has been taken ill. He needs rest. I want you and Richard to stay your distance today and remain quiet."

The curtain to Aunt Emma's room was pulled back and in their bed lay Papa. "Is it the epidemic?" asked Jenny anxiously.

Aunt Emma who was making a cup of tea, handed it to Mamma who went back to Papa's side. "Brendan doesn't believe it to be the epidemic, but it is better to be safe. Your papa's got the shakes and fever. We think it's just the ague."

Jenny watched from behind the curtain as Mamma tried to give Papa some of the warm tea. He thrashed around in the bed and upset the cup of tea in Mamma's lap.

Just then Richard came down the kitchen steps carrying a bucket of rainwater from the barrel on the deck. He motioned for Jenny to follow him back up on the deck.

"I know what it is. I saw it before," said Richard. "In the woods there are plants that'll help. The feverwort, dogwood, and hops all help with fever, ague, and malaria. I got to go get some if your pa is to get better."

"You better tell Mamma or Uncle McKee."

"I already told McKee. He told me to keep my mumbo-jumbo to myself and stay aboard."

"When will you be back?" asked Jenny.

"I'll be back when I find what I need. You tell 'em I'll be back. You be strong. Your ma needs your help now. Remember what the old woman said; life is good if you don't weaken."

Jenny nodded as she fought back the tears.

"I'll find you along the canal as soon as I can. Be strong." Seeing his chance to escape unnoticed, Richard slipped over the side of the boat into the canal. He held his breath and dipped beneath the water as the *William and Mary* moved on.

Jenny watched Richard swim to the bank and then went below and sat with Aunt Emma. Behind the curtain Mamma held Papa's hand as he slept and occasionally wiped his head with a cool cloth.

"Your papa'll be fine. He's a strong man. The fever won't take him," Aunt Emma reassured Jenny.

Needing something to do, Jenny found the sewing basket and the quilt her mother had started for Aunt Emma's baby. She started to piece together two of the quilt squares, both scraps from dresses she had outgrown.

"I know that quilt was intended for my baby," Aunt Emma smiled. "But you'll be leaving soon, and when you get to the Territory there'll be no time for quilting. So I want you to finish it after you're settled and put it in your trunk to have when you get married. It'll be kind of a gift from me to you for your wedding day."

"But I'm still going to try to get it done for you and the baby," Jenny promised.

Emma patted Jenny's hand just as Mamma entered the kitchen. "Come sit, sister," urged Emma. "You need the rest. You were up almost the whole night. Jenny and I will look after him."

"No, I don't want you two to catch whatever it is. I'll be fine."

Jenny got up from the table and brought Mamma some tea and a piece of bread with jam.

"Thank you. I'm glad to see you're finally doing your needlework."

Jenny sat and selected some more cloth pieces from the basket.

"You remember all this material? Most of it came from your old dresses. The scraps will make a pretty quilt for the baby if it's a girl. I remember the quilt our mamma made for Emma before she was born."

Emma took Mamma's hand. "Don't be fretting, sister. He'll get better."

Mamma hung her head and tears flowed down her cheeks. "What will we do if something happens to him, Emma? What will we do?"

Aunt Emma put her arm around Mamma.

"Papa will be all right once Richard gets back," blurted Jenny.

"Where'd that boy go?" asked Emma sharply.

"He went to gather medicine plants."

"Oh, mercy. Husband will be upset. He already told him he wasn't to be leaving the *William and Mary* today."

"How will he ever catch up with us?" asked Mamma.

"He's a fast runner. He said he'd be back. He gave his word."

Mamma stood with a sigh and walked silently back to Papa's side.

"You shouldn't have said anything. Your mamma doesn't need any more worries."

"I thought it would make her feel better," said Jenny sadly.

"I know, dear. You meant well." Emma picked up the sewing basket and started to sort through the material. "Look. This looks like the pattern in your sunbonnet. It's green with pink flowers. I do like that bonnet of yours. You make sure you always wear it when you're in the Territory. It will keep you from turning old before your time."

Jenny and Aunt Emma worked together on the quilt for several hours. At dinner time Aunt Emma made sandwiches. Mamma only nibbled at hers and returned quickly to Papa's side.

Jenny took a sandwich to Uncle McKee who ate as he stood at the tiller."Mighty quiet around here. Where's the boy? Ain't seen him around since morning."

"He went to get plants to help Papa."

"He left the boat without permission? That boy is trouble. I don't think he'll come back. First signs of sickness, most people run scared. They think it's the epidemic again."

"He'll be back. He gave his word."

"His word? He was raised in the swamp, girl. His word means next to nothin'. I hope you said your goodbyes to that one."

"I don't believe it. He wouldn't lie. He said he was going for medicine plants and would be back as soon as he found them."

"And when did he say that?"

Jenny paused for a moment. "This morning."

"See. The woods are full of plants. He would have found what he needed by now."

"He said they were special plants. He had to get the right ones."

"I'll believe it when I see it," Uncle snapped.

The rest of the afternoon Jenny helped as much as she could and worked on the quilt to help keep her mind off Papa and Richard. By supper Richard still hadn't returned. Perhaps Uncle McKee was right, Jenny thought sadly.

After the *William and Mary* stopped for the evening Uncle McKee called Jenny to come to the deck. "Look who's coming up the towpath," he said as he pointed. There trudged Richard with his arms full of plants and his dog following.

"Guess I was wrong. I owe you an apology for making you worry," offered Uncle McKee.

Jenny hopped off the boat and ran to meet Richard. His clothes were muddy and his arms and face scratched. "I found what I needed, but I had to go a ways. How's your pa?"

"He's the same. Burning with fever and then shaking." Jenny took some of the plants as the two boarded the *William and Mary*.

"Boy, ya look like ya fought with a panther," said Uncle. "Why don't you clean up and get a bite to eat. Give that wolf of yours something, too."

A smile spread across Richard's face. "Thanks. I did get a little tangled in a thicket and I'm right hungry to boot."

Down in the kitchen Richard and Jenny put the plants in a bucket of cool water.

"What's this?" asked Aunt Emma.

"It's medicine plants. They'll help the fever. We have to boil 'em up, strain 'em, and give 'em to him like broth," said Richard.

Exhausted and nervous, Mamma came from Papa's side. "I don't want any swamp medicine."

"But this will help. The old woman used to make it all the time for the canal men. They got the same fever."

Raising her voice Mamma repeated, "I don't want swamp medicine!"

Uncle McKee came down the stairs to the kitchen. "What's the trouble?"

"She don't want the medicine," Richard said sadly as he hung his head.

"What if it kills him?" cried Mamma in a fearful way as she grabbed the curtain to help her stand.

Aunt Emma rushed to Mamma's side and helped her to the bench. "You're just too tired to think straight. You need rest."

"Swamp medicine can help," said Uncle McKee. "It won't hurt him none. I've seen it before. The boy's right. See here, he's got hops. Boiled into a broth it'll bring down the fever. Same with feverwort. He'll be better by mornin'."

"But what if it kills him?" Mamma cried.

Aunt Emma put her arm around Mamma and guided her to the back cabin. "Sister, I want you to rest."

"Boy, you go wash up and eat," instructed McKee. "Jenny and I will clean up these plants. When you finish you can tell us what to do next. Don't forget to feed that wolf of yours either."

Jenny looked at her uncle in surprise.

"What ya lookin' at, girl? I know this medicine works. I lived my whole life along the canal. My pa's life was saved by this stuff. Let's get to work. Time's a- wastin'."

Richard ate quickly and filled a bowl with scraps for the dog.

"Put the bowl on the deck. Emma wouldn't like it none if one of her bowls was to be lost on the path. The dog can eat on board."

Richard returned quickly and the three began boiling the medicine. It was nearly midnight when McKee helped Richard strain the hot liquid so that it was ready for Papa.

Uncle McKee stood when Mamma returned to the kitchen from her rest. "I took it upon myself to have the boy make up the medicine. I thought when you awoke I might convince you. Case's fever hasn't come down, and I'm afraid it'll weaken him to a point where. . .."

"I know," interrupted Mamma softly. Walking to the boy she put her arms around him. "Please forgive me," she whispered. "And thank you for getting the plants."

Richard smiled. "It's ready if you can get him to take some." Pouring some of the hot liquid into a bowl to cool he handed it to Mamma along with a spoon. "Try to give all of this to him if you can."

For a long time Mamma spooned small amounts of medicine into Papa's mouth. Then she sat by his side while the others slept in the kitchen and back cabin.

Just before sunrise Jenny heard Mamma call, "Quick! Everyone come here!"

Jenny ran to the curtained bedroom with Richard and Uncle McKee following.

"It's over. The fever broke!"

Papa lay there with his eyes open, smiling weakly. "McKee," he said hoarsely, "what are you doing? Sitting a **wake**?"

Uncle laughed and joined Mamma by the bedside. Mamma reached out to Richard and squeezed his hand. "It worked. I'm **beholden** to you."

"Papa, Richard made swamp medicine out of plants. He brought down your fever. He saved your life," Jenny could hardly say enough about her friend's skills.

"Ya got a good one here, Case," said Uncle. "He'll be mighty handy in the Territory."

Papa smiled up at Richard, "Thank you, son."

Papa ate bread and milk and soon went back to sleep. Mamma, too tired to eat, lay down in the back cabin and slept most of the morning. Up on the deck the dog sat peacefully and watched McKee, Richard, and Jenny take turns at the tiller steering the *William and Mary.*

It was noon when the town of Lockport came into view. Boats lined the waterway, waiting their turn to enter the Lockport Five. This double series of five locks had been built end-to-end so that boats could be moved up or down a huge rocky ridge.

Bumping along the stone wall, the *William and Mary* moved into the first lock. Water filled the lock until the boat was raised twelve feet. It was then moved into a second lock and raised twelve feet more to the third lock. To Jenny it seemed as if the boat was ever so slowly climbing a huge water stairway. It took three hours for the boat to move through the five locks. When they were released from the fifth lock into the western section of the canal they were sixty feet higher than where they had started.

That evening Papa was feeling better and joined the family at supper. "After hearing what the old man had to say about Toledo," he suggested, "I think we might be wise to take the steamboat to Detroit."

"Smart thinking," agreed Uncle McKee. "I was gonna suggest the same thing when you were well enough again. The cost will be higher for the steamer, but it is better to be safe."

"Than sorry," added Richard.

"Well, that does it then. We all agree," said Papa.

Jenny noticed that only the men agreed. The women were never asked.

"When should we start packing?" asked Mamma softly, knowing she would soon be saying goodbye to Emma.

"We'll be there by late tomorrow morning," said McKee.

"Jenny and I will pack," said Mamma. "You, husband, need your rest so you will have your strength when we reach the Territory."

"I'll rest on the steamboat," said Papa. "We have a three-day voyage on Lake Erie, and there can't be much to do on a steamboat."

"I'll help pack," offered Richard. "Just think, I'm going west!"

Uncle McKee took a piece of bread and wiped his plate clean. He then broke it into small pieces and scattered it over his plate. Seeing everyone watching he commented, "It's for the wolf. Excuse me, the dog." He exited up the stairs with Richard following.

"Don't be feeding the dog on my good plate," protested Emma.

Papa laughed. "I think I should have gotten sick sooner. It seems to have helped everyone's disposition."

Jenny followed Papa as he climbed into bed. "Papa, Richard is going with us to the Territory, isn't he?"

"Well, of course. He's part of the family now."

"Papa, do they let dogs come on steamers?"

"Well, I don't know. I hadn't thought about that."

"You know, Richard won't come without the dog," Jenny said quietly.

Up on the deck McKee spoke with Richard. "You know, boy, ya can't be takin' that wolf of yours on a steamer. They won't allow it."

"She ain't a wolf, she's a dog."

"Well, she looks enough like a wolf, and they won't allow it. If you want, you can leave her with me. I'll look after her for you. And Emma has taken a shine to her."

Richard stood and shook his head. "I'm not leaving her. She's my friend. I couldn't leave her."

"Now see here, boy, there's no way they'll let ya bring her on board the steamer. And I'm willing to help you. Don't be foolish. Think about it."

Richard sat on the deck for a long time, his arms wrapped around the dog. He couldn't leave her. He just couldn't.

Chapter 8
A Real Wild Cat!

It was late morning by the time the *William and Mary* reached Buffalo. The traffic along the canal had increased as freight boats and line boats passed them heading east to Albany with their goods.

Papa had regained much of his strength. He carefully organized the trunks, boxes, barrels, and carpetbags. He checked to see if their seeds were still dry and ran them through his fingers. "This is our future," he said to Jenny. "Good New York seeds to plant in the Territory soil. There's no better combination."

As soon as the boat was tied Papa and Uncle McKee left to book passage to Detroit on the steamer *United States*. Shortly after Jenny noticed that Richard and the dog were also gone. She watched along the canal, hoping they had just gone for a walk. But when dinner was served, Richard still wasn't there and Jenny, Mamma, and Emma had all begun to worry.

When Papa and McKee returned to the boat two hours later Papa waved four tickets in his hand. "Our tickets to the Territory," he said as he picked Mamma up high and twirled her around. He then began to pack their supplies into a small wagon he rented. "Where's Richard," he asked. "I need his help."

Papa turned and saw the worried look on Mamma's face. "What's wrong," he asked.

"The boy's gone. We can't find him anywhere. He's just up and vanished—with the dog."

Papa hopped up on the bank of the canal. "Maybe he's just out exploring. You know how the boy is."

"I don't think so," said Emma.

"It's the dog, Papa," said Jenny sadly. "He couldn't take the dog so they ran away."

"We've got our tickets," said Papa. "We'll be leaving by late afternoon." Silently he and McKee loaded the wagon.

The long walk to the steamer allowed the family to search the crowds for Richard. At the docks steamboats and sailboats arrived hourly. Buffalo was obviously a place of transit for both people and products. There were piles of freight and furniture, and everywhere people seemed to be searching for goods or waiting for boats.

As they stood near the *United States* Mamma and Emma held hands and hugged until a shrill whistle blew so loudly that everyone jumped. McKee slapped

Papa on the back and kissed Mamma. "Girl,' he said as he turned to Jenny, "the next time I see you you'll probably be a bride." Bending down, he kissed Jenny softly on the cheek.

"Case, I'll keep an eye out for that boy of yours. If he shows up along the canal, I'll bring him and that wolf of his to the Territory myself. I'm sure Emma wouldn't mind paying a visit to her sister." Aunt Emma took Uncle McKee by the arm and squeezed it tightly.

Mamma, Jenny, and Papa boarded the *United States* with other people headed west. Then, struggling under its great load of passengers and freight, the steamer made its way out into the harbor, its smokestacks belching huge gray clouds of smoke. The short and choppy waves of Lake Erie rocked the heavy steamer along its way. It was headed west to the Michigan Territory.

After he was satisfied that all their belongings were together and safely stored, Papa led Mamma and Jenny to the lower deck to find their cabin. Winding their way through the freight and stacks of wood needed to fuel the boat, the three entered a tiny cabin with a small bed.

While Mamma worried how they would sleep in the tiny space, Jenny went up on deck and looked back toward the harbor. Papa followed, knowing she was thinking about Richard. "He'll be all right. Your uncle will see to that."

Jenny looked up at Papa and nodded, but she still wished Richard was with them.

As they finally cleared the harbor the steamer's shrill whistle sounded again. Jenny thought she heard a familiar sound accompanying the whistle.

"What's wrong?" asked Papa, seeing the look on her face.

"Oh, nothing," said Jenny.

Satisfied that Jenny was okay, Papa returned to the cabin. Jenny stayed on deck, watching the big lake open up before them. It was the first time she had ever seen so much water. This must be like the ocean, she thought.

On the lake there were other steamers passing. Each time they passed each other, they signaled a greeting with their loud shrill whistles. And each time a whistle blew, Jenny heard the same familiar sound. Was it just her imagination, or was it a dog's howl?

Soon Jenny's curiosity got the best of her and she began to wander around the deck, hoping to find the source of the noise. She followed some stairs down to an open storage area. There in the dim light she could see barrels, trunks, furniture, and baskets stored for the trip to the Michigan Territory. It seemed to her that the sound had come from this area, but she found no clues.

Just as Jenny headed back up the stairs, the steamboat's whistle blew again. This time it was accompanied by an unmistakable howl! Quickly she made her way through the freight and boxes, following the sound to the back of the storage room. There she saw what she had hardly dared hope for—Richard and the dog!

When Richard spied Jenny a big grin covered his face. "You 'bout scared the life out of me, girl. What are you doing sneaking up on us like that?"

Jenny climbed over a set of crates to the pair and wrapped her arms around them. "I thought you ran away. I thought you left us. How did you get here?"

Richard pushed Jenny back. "I ain't stupid. I'm going west with ya!"

"But how did you get here? I've got to tell Papa." Jenny began to stand and Richard grabbed her arm.

"You can't tell him. He wouldn't like it none. Your pa's a righteous man. He wouldn't like it that I'm a **stowaway**. Tell him when we get to Detroit. It'll be a good surprise then."

"But Papa bought you a ticket. You're supposed to be here."

"He bought me a ticket? But my dog—he couldn't buy a ticket for my dog. I knew I'd have to leave her, and I just couldn't do that."

Jenny nodded.

"I waited this mornin' and followed your pa and McKee to the docks so I could find out what steamer you were gonna take. Then when freight started to be loaded, I snuck aboard. I thought I'd surprise ya in Detroit."

"How were you going to eat? You don't even have water?"

"We've been hungry and thirsty before. Besides, this ol' Lake Erie can't be all that big to cross."

"It's big all right. Three days big."

Just then someone called from the entrance to the storage room. "Who's in there?"

Richard grabbed the dog and put his hands around her muzzle to keep her quiet. Jenny ducked and remained silent.

"Who's there?" the voice called again. "I heard ya and I'm coming back to get ya. Might as well show yourself."

Jenny whispered to Richard. "I'll be back," and crept toward the middle of the room.

"I'm in here," Jenny called as she stood. "I'm Jenny Case and I am just checking our supplies."

The man who worked on the boat stood blinking into the dim light. "You get yourself out of here, girl. This is no place to be playing."

"I wasn't playing. I was checking our supplies, making sure you got them all. We're going to the Territory and we need all we brought."

Jenny made her way through the freight toward the entrance. "You did a good job. It appears everything is here."

"Mighty sassy for a girl," said the man as she passed him and started up the stairs.

As Jenny came on deck, Papa spied her with the man.

"Jenny, what's going on?"

"I found her below," said the man.

"I was just checking our supplies," Jenny said as she stared at Papa in a strange way.

Papa frowned and stammered, "Well, is it all there, daughter?"

"They did a fine job," responded Jenny.

"It's nice to see people who do their work properly," said Papa as he reached out and patted the man on the shoulder. The man smiled and walked away, proud of the compliment.

As soon as the man had disappeared, Papa asked, "What in tarnation is going on?"

"I can't say."

"You better say, young lady. What were you doing below?"

"I gave my word. I can't say."

"Who'd you give your word to?"

Just then the steamer passed another boat and sounded its shrill horn. And as they stood at the top of the stairs, Papa also heard the howl from below.

"Tarnation! You don't mean to tell me that the boy's down there with the dog?"

"He told me not to tell you. He couldn't leave her so he stowed away with the freight."

Papa drove his hands deep into his pockets and walked to the ship's railing.

"He told me not to tell. What are you going to do, Papa?"

Papa was silent for a moment. Then he looked at Jenny and shrugged his shoulders. "Me? I won't do a thing. I paid the boy's passage. They've got my money. I'll do nothing. But he will have to stay below with that—pet of his."

"I told him I'd bring him food and water," said Jenny.

"What about a blanket? Does he have a blanket?"

Jenny didn't know.

"He'll need that, too. He will have to stay below during daylight hours. He can come out on the deck at night to take a stretch.

"You tell him that. You also tell him he'd better clean up after he brings the dog on deck or they'll know what he's about.

"Tell him also to keep silent down there even when the whistle blows. I'd hate to think what would happen if they discover her and mistake her for a wolf."

Jenny listened carefully to all that Papa said, trying to remember everything to tell Richard. That night she brought food and water below, being careful not to get caught. And much later, when everyone had gone to their cabins, Richard and the dog crept up to the deck for a short stretch.

On the third day, the steamer sounded its whistle as it approached the harbor at Detroit, the capital city of the Territory. Jenny thought this was the biggest and prettiest town she had ever seen.

At the docks Jenny, Papa, and Mamma watched anxiously as their boxes, trunks, and barrels were unloaded. But Richard and the dog were nowhere to be seen. After awhile Papa decided to go and make arrangements to buy a covered wagon and team for their trip into the Territory. "Time's a-wasting. That boy can't keep holding us up," said Papa as he walked down the muddy road to a nearby stable and barn.

Soon he returned with a team of horses and a large wagon. Arching over the wagon bed was a series of wooden hoops. A white canvas top was roped and drawn taut over the hoops.

"This will be our home for a few days," said Papa as he and Mamma admired the wagon's full, round lines.

Just then Jenny felt a nudge on her leg. She looked down and saw the dog. Jenny stooped and wrapped her arms around its neck.

"Don't I get anything for being so smart?" came a voice. It was Richard.

"Smart? You're lucky you didn't get thrown off the boat," said Jenny as she reached out and kissed Richard on the cheek.

"Stop that! Why do girls always kiss?"

Papa came around the side of the wagon with Mamma. He patted Richard and gave him a big hug. Mamma hugged Richard, too, giving him another kiss on the cheek.

"Welcome to the Territory," said Papa loudly. "Let's get loaded."

Jenny and Mamma handed smaller boxes to Papa and Richard as they filled the inside of the wagon. When everything was loaded, they moved the wagon to a public well near the docks and filled the water barrels that were attached to the side of the wagon.

Checking to see if everything was in order, Richard walked around the wagon and straight into a dirty, mean-looking man.

"Well, looky here, brother," the man said to a companion that followed. "I think we got ourselves some settler folks."

Just then the dog rounded the wagon with a low growl.

"Hey, looks like we got us a tame wolf, too. Ain't seen no better pelt than this one in awhile."

Jenny froze and stared at the two men, both of them dirty and scraggly with rotten teeth. One carried a rifle and the other had a long knife hanging from his belt.

Richard pulled the dog close to him. "She ain't no wolf. She's a dog. Look at her eyes."

"It's a shame these settler folks made a pet of this here wolf," said the man with the long knife. "It'll make it all that harder to skin that pretty hide off it."

Papa drew near, putting his hand on Richard's shoulder. "Why don't you be tending your own business and we'll be moving on," he said firmly.

"Brother, what would you say? Would you say killin' a wolf in the Territory is our business?"

The other man spit a dirty, brown stream of tobacco juice at Papa's feet and laughed. "Yankee, wolf huntin' is our business."

Mamma, who had quietly climbed to the seat of the wagon, quickly searched through the packed goods for her broom. Sliding down from the seat, she flew around the edge of the wagon swinging her broom high in the air and bringing it down with a crash on top of the first man's head.

"You get yourselves out of here, you dirty, nasty,

trouble-making animals!" With each name she slapped and swatted the men with her broom.

Shocked, Papa grabbed Mamma around the waist. "Woman, stop!"

Mamma's hairpins flew as she struggled with Papa. Her hair stuck out from its roll on the top of her head and she still tried to hit the men with the broom.

"Get away from here, you two mongrels. Leave my family alone!"

The men, shocked and uncertain if Mamma was crazy, turned and trotted up the street, looking back over their shoulders. "We should've been huntin' wildcats, brother," one called, " 'cause there's a good one right here on the streets of Dee-troit."

Mamma collapsed into Papa's arms, dropping her broom. "I'm a Territory wife now," she puffed as she pushed her hair back out of her eyes. "I can't be a weak one, and sometimes a broom is a better answer than a gun."

"In my estimation, wife," said Papa, "it appears you did a right fine job of sweeping."

The four of them burst into a relieved laughter.

Chapter 9
Detroit

After Mamma settled down and pulled her hair neatly back into a bun, she put her sunbonnet on her head and handed Jenny hers. Turning to Richard she instructed, "Put the dog into the wagon until we've passed through this place. These people are either wild men or citified. And neither likes the looks of that pet of yours."

Papa agreed and Richard boosted the dog into the wagon. The entire family climbed aboard and Papa steered the team away from the docks of Lake Erie and onto Woodbridge Road.

The wheels of the heavily loaded wagon cut deep tracks into the mud as they moved toward the heart of the city. Along a street named after Thomas Jefferson, there were stands selling fresh fruits, vegetables, and meats. Papa stopped to purchase enough supplies to feed them until they settled into their new homestead.

Jenny and Richard laughed as they observed the many different types of people who had come together in this place called Detroit. Some wore buckskin and carried rifles; others wore tall wide-brimmed hats and dark suits. There were Indians wrapped in blankets and ladies in silk dresses with feathered bonnets.

"This here town's laid out like a big wheel," said a man who came back to the wagon helping Papa. The man rolled a barrel of potatoes on the muddy street and lifted it into the wagon. Papa carried an open box filled with onions, carrots, turnips, and rutabagas.

Richard and Jenny listened as they talked. "These streets all come together like a hub of a wheel. You can find our capitol building on Griswold Street, just up the road a bit. And if you keep going north by northwest out of town, you'll soon come to the trail you're looking for. You can't miss it."

Papa thanked the man for his help and directions. As the wagon moved away, the man waved and called, "Welcome to the Territory, folks."

By late afternoon, Papa had found the north fork of the Grand River Trail heading west out of Detroit. They were finally on the road to their new wilderness home.

The first few miles along the trail was bordered by a line of farms, fields, and places where the axe was making war with the trees. On each side of the trail there lay deep water-filled ditches separating them from the wilderness.

As they moved on there were long stretches of forest where only a few cabins dotted the way. Here and there, Jenny and Richard noticed piles of black, smoking logs where the land was being cleared. "Lots of work will be needed before this land is captured from the wilderness," said Papa, pointing to the log piles.

When there were no longer cabins in sight, Richard let the dog out from her confined quarters. He and Jenny jumped down, following the wagon as it jolted back and forth on the rutted road.

As the sun began to set, Papa decided they should make camp. Mamma, concerned that Papa's fever might return if he didn't rest, agreed.

Just as they began watching for a good place to camp along the trail, the outline of a cabin loomed ahead of them. "Now that is a truly wonderful sight. It must be the inn the man told me about. I was worried we might already be lost." Papa laughed as Mamma gave him a sharp poke with her elbow.

"This will be the last chance we have to sleep inside for awhile," he continued. "I suggest we spend the night."

Papa pulled the wagon around behind the inn to the stables and he and Richard unhitched the horses. Mamma took Jenny by the hand and led the way into the inn. Since it was still early in the evening, she was able to secure a room that didn't have to be shared with strangers.

The room was small but had two beds covered with clean quilts and a washstand with towels, a large pitcher of water, and basin. A small mirror hung on the wall. Mamma poured water into the basin and washed her hands and face. When she finished, Jenny did the same.

Soon Richard and Papa appeared in the doorway, stomping mud and manure off their feet. Papa, more tired than Jenny had ever seen him, sat on one of the beds while Richard washed.

"Well, son, I hope you don't mind sharing a bed with me tonight."

Smiling, Richard looked up at Papa. "If you don't snore any louder than my dog, I don't see it to be a problem."

With a grin Papa rose and shared the wash basin with Richard. When they had washed and combed their hair the four went downstairs for supper.

By this time many travelers had gathered at the long tables in the dining room. The innkeeper served hard biscuits, **johnny cakes** with syrup, **salt pork**, and buttermilk. Richard and Papa finished first and were served great pieces of pie. Richard, who had seldom tasted desserts, gulped his down.

As they finished their meal, two men at the end of the table talked loudly about the Toledo War. They laughed and snickered about it being called a war. "There weren't no bloodshed, 'cept some Michigan deputy sheriff stabbed with a pocketknife during a drunken brawl."

Others joined in telling funny stories they had heard about the war. "It shoulda been called the Chicken War," said one man, "with all the chicken-thieving that went on along the border."

"What about that dead horse?" said another.

"That weren't no horse. That were a mule."

"I heard it was a pig," joined another. The longer the men talked the louder they got and the more they laughed.

Suddenly the loud talking and laughing quieted as a low, lonesome howl came from outside. It was Richard's dog. Richard reached across the table for a handful of biscuits and shoved them into his pockets. "She wants her supper, I guess."

One of the men at the end of the table glanced out the window. "Who wants to go wolf hunting tonight? I sure could use the **bounty**," Several other men cheered.

Richard leaned to talk with Papa, "I best be sleepin' in the wagon with the dog tonight." Papa nodded. Richard left the dining room and headed directly to the stables where the dog greeted him and quickly gulped down the biscuits.

By the first morning light, Papa was already dressed and in the dining room. By the time Mamma and Jenny were ready, Papa had taken Richard and the dog some bread and slices of cold ham and was harnessing the horses. Richard put the dog safely in the wagon, drawing down the canvas so that she could not be seen.

By the time the sun was peeking through the trees, the Case wagon was winding down the narrow trail into the wilderness. Several times Papa pointed out deer that bounded across the trail and disappeared into the tangled woods. Richard, Jenny, and the dog jumped from the wagon and walked behind it as it wobbled back and forth on the rutted road. Here and there the travelers came upon **oak openings**, streams, or small lakes.

At dinnertime Papa stopped the wagon to rest the horses. Mamma served biscuits and cold baked potatoes she had brought from the inn. They drank water from a small nearby stream.

Although it was good to rest and eat, everyone soon realized the flies would not let them stay for long. They covered everything that wasn't moving and swarmed around Jenny and the others. By the time the family was back on the trail they were covered with red welts.

By nightfall Papa estimated they had traveled at least twenty miles. Jenny and Richard collected fire-wood and Papa built a fine fire. From the back of the wagon Mamma brought out a skillet and coffee pot that had been packed in the kitchen barrel. "It's nice to see these things again," she said as she remembered her cozy kitchen in New York State.

Papa and Richard unpacked blankets and quilts and made a large bed under the wagon. The black flies that had bothered them so at dinner were now replaced by swarms of mosquitoes. Jenny thought that they were larger than any she had ever seen.

Battling mosquitoes as she worked, Jenny washed potatoes and put them on sticks. Then she pushed the sticks into the ground near the fire so that the potatoes would roast. Meanwhile Mamma fried salt pork in her skillet.

As soon as supper was ready, Papa put green wood on the fire to create smoke and drive away the blood-thirsty mosquitoes while they ate. With smoke stinging their eyes, they ate quickly. The dog sat nearby, snapping both at mosquitoes and any scraps the family threw her.

After supper Jenny cleaned the dishes while Papa and Richard gathered more firewood. "I thought we would be leaving in the morning," said Mamma, "but it looks like you got wood enough to stay a week."

"Better to have too much than not enough," said Papa. "Besides, there will be settlers coming down the trail who will be happy to have the wood ready for their cooking fires." Mamma smiled at her husband's generous nature.

That night the fire was built high and sparks flew into the great trees that surrounded them. Richard, holding his dog tightly by the nape of its neck, sat beside Papa and talked about their new home.

Mamma moved closer to the fire and wrapped herself and Jenny in her shawl.

From the distance came the haunting sound of a wolf howl as the darkness grew deeper. Soon another howl echoed through the air and an eerie choir of wolves sang in the darkness. The hair on the back of the dog's neck stood tall and goose bumps formed on Jenny's arms. Richard held the dog closely to him as her ears twitched and she sniffed the air.

"You'll have to be watching her close," said Papa. "I understand these wolves travel in packs bigger than any seen in New York. There could be dozens of them out there. They'll either rip her to pieces or persuade her to run with them."

Papa put more wood on the fire and poked the embers until the flames snapped and crackled high into the air. The fire cast a huge light around the wagon. But just beyond the light, red eyes glowed in the shadows as the wolves stood watching the fire when they were not howling or growling at each other.

"Should we sleep in the wagon?" asked Mamma.

"There's not room enough," Papa answered, "and besides, there's no protection in the wagon if those critters would come over here. We need to be near the fire. Under the wagon will be fine."

Trying to be strong, Mamma held Jenny's hand, but Jenny could feel her shaking with fright.

"Don't you go worrying none," said Papa. "I'll keep the fire up. Those wolves won't bother us close up to camp."

Mamma, still holding Jenny's hand, decided it was time for bed. Together they crawled under the wagon and pulled the soft, warm quilts over their heads.

Concerned about the dog, Papa cut a long rope and handed it to Richard. "I want you to make a collar and tie that dog to the wagon wheel. If she runs into the forest, we will never see her again."

Richard knew this was true. He knotted a loop around the dog's neck and tied the rope tightly to the spokes of the wagon wheel.

It seemed to Jenny that she lay awake for hours and hours listening to the wolves howl and fight. Papa puffed on his pipe as he kept watch, keeping his rifle at his side. Richard took turns with Papa so that he could doze by the fire. Although he was tired and worried about losing his dog in the wilderness, the boy was still glad he was finally heading west.

By sunrise everyone was still tired from their restless, noisy night. The wolves were silent now, sleeping somewhere in the forest after their long night of welcoming new settlers.

Everyone moved slowly. Jenny helped Mamma make cornmeal **mush**. Papa gulped cups of hot coffee, trying to regain his energy. Richard helped Papa pack away quilts and ready the horses and wagon for the day's journey.

As they pulled away from camp, Jenny and Richard quietly walked the trail. The dog trailed behind, tied to the wagon. Soon the land became low and marshy and the trail turned into a **corduroy road** that led them through a dense, swampy forest. It was not a cheery place, and huge swarms of flies and mosquitoes accompanied the travelers.

Papa tried to direct the wagon to the smoothest part of the logged trail. Still, the wagon bumped and jarred along. It lurched forward when the front wheels went over the logs and then swung backward when the rear wheels went over. It also swayed from side to side, threatening to tip over.

Mamma held tightly to the edge of her seat, fearing that at any moment she could be thrown off.

"Looks like others have come this way to make this road so smooth," Papa teased.

Mamma nodded and prayed her husband knew what he was doing. Jenny and Richard, both barefooted, picked their way along the muddy, log-covered trail. The dog, now released from her rope, jumped over big muddy ruts and lapped water from their holes.

The swamp took three hours to cross and by the time they pulled out of the muck and mire, Mamma was shaken to pieces. She begged Papa to stop the wagon and when he did, she slid from her seat and shook off her mud-covered skirts.

Looking back she spied Jenny and Richard coming along the trail with the dog. When she realized Jenny was barefooted and had her skirts pulled high, Mamma had a fit. "Husband, what are we going to do with this girl? She soon will be as wild as the wilderness itself."

Papa smiled. "I wouldn't worry. I am sure she will become a lady like her mother. After all, she has you to teach her. As for being barefooted, I think she showed common sense. There is no reason to ruin her boots in all this mud."

Thinking for a moment, Mamma agreed. "But what about her skirts? A lady never pulls her skirts up to her knees."

Papa laughed and helped Mamma back onto her seat. "Now just you stop fretting. We'll soon be safe and snug in our own home, and you can get on with your manner-learning then. Besides—I did notice she was wearing her sunbonnet." Papa smiled and kissed Mamma's hand.

"Mr. Case, you are a charmer," she said as the wagon moved forward.

At a clearing up the trail, they stopped again and Mamma fixed a quick dinner of leftover mush and crackers, just enough to fill their empty stomachs. In a nearby stream Jenny washed her feet. At Mamma's instructions she put on her boots and promised to keep her skirts lower, "like a lady."

The afternoon passed peacefully as the wagon moved along a dry, smooth trail. At nightfall, Papa and Richard again built a bright fire and sat watch. It seemed to Jenny that the wolves moved even closer to camp, or that her family was moving deeper into the wolves' territory. The animals snarled and snapped in the surrounding darkness. Their ghostly howls and red glaring eyes were everywhere. The dog strained at her rope as she snarled and howled back. Richard checked many times to make sure the rope was tied tightly.

By morning the family was exhausted once again. Although the trail was clear and dry, the sun beat down. Papa stopped several times so that they could cool themselves in nearby streams.

Late in the afternoon Papa pointed to a small log cabin off the trail. "Put the dog in the wagon," he instructed.

Just then an old man came from the cabin and called down the trail. "Ya want lodgin'?" he asked as he chewed on the stem of a corncob pipe.

"If it can be had," called Papa. "It would sure be a relief from sleeping with the wolves."

The man chuckled, understanding what Papa meant. "Come on in. Pull the wagon around back."

Leaving Papa and Richard to unhitch the horses, Mamma and Jenny approached the cabin. The front door opened slightly, and there stood a pretty little girl with bright blue eyes and a dirt-streaked face. Her long hair was snarled and looked as if it had never been brushed.

"Look, Jenny," said Mamma. "Maybe you can make a friend."

The old man spoke up. "Can't make a friend with that one. She can't hear or speak either."

Just then the door opened fully and a dirty young woman appeared. "This here's my wife."

Mamma looked at Jenny and took her hand. This woman is young enough to be the man's daughter—maybe even his granddaughter, thought Jenny.

"Go on in," the man pointed to the cabin.

"Can we wash up first?" asked Mamma. "It's been a mighty hot, dirty day."

"Over there's the rain barrel. On the bench is a pot and a rag," he said pointing to the side of the cabin.

Mamma and Jenny dipped water from the rain barrel into the pot and removing their bonnets, washed their hands and faces. The rag, dirtier than they ever were, hung on a bush by the bench.

"Let's just let nature dry us," whispered Mamma. Jenny thought it was a good idea.

When they went into the cabin, they found it very dark with only a dirt floor. The woman swung a cooking pot out from the fireplace and began dishing up bowls of thick stew. The little girl pushed dirt and crumbs off the table, making a place for Mamma and Jenny to sit and eat.

As the woman dished out the stew, she paused and spit into the fire. Mamma's eyes grew large and then she turned away. "I don't know if I can eat, but you may if you wish," Mamma said quietly to Jenny so as not to hurt the woman's feelings.

When Papa, Richard, and the man came in the woman handed them bowls of stew. The man, who hadn't had company for some time, talked as he stuffed his mouth with food. Jenny watched as he chewed, slurped, and talked all at the same time. The stew dribbled down his chin and onto his dirty beard and shirt.

After talking about the weather, the road, and politics, the man changed his conversation to religion. "Religion is like fashion to me," he said.

Mamma looked up and stared at him in disbelief.

He continued, "One man wears his jacket buttoned, another wears it laced, and still another plain, but every man has a jacket. So every man has his religion. Today in this new world in the wilderness, every man has his way of observing."

"But surely the good book has its place in the wilderness," Mamma interrupted.

"That's true, woman," the man responded, "but ya hafta be able to read to know what's in the book."

Looking at Mamma he instructed, "Eat, woman. It's the best you'll be getting."

Ashamed of her behavior, Mamma looked shyly at Papa. "Eat. It's very good."

Mamma and Jenny tasted their stew. It really was very good. The dirty young woman smiled at Mamma with pride, half of her teeth already missing. "It's possum stew," she said. "Just made it yesterday. It ain't turned yet."

Mamma smiled and ate slowly.

The little girl sat beside Jenny and slurped down a bowl of stew. At the fire the young woman turned and spit a long brown stream of tobacco juice into the flames. The spit sizzled on the logs and a puff of stinky gray smoke dissolved into the air.

Looking away, Mamma continued eating.

The young woman then came to the table with a corncob pipe. She nudged Mamma on the arm. "Ya can smoke if ya like."

"No thanks," said Mamma, trying to hide her surprise.

"Me neither. I prefer ta chew," she said with a smile and joined them at the table to eat.

Richard, who had eaten his fill, grinned at Jenny. "The ole woman in the swamps used to chew." He stood up from the table. "Well, if you don't mind I'll be spending an early night in the wagon." Shortly after he left, Papa and the old man followed.

Jenny thought that sleeping in the wagon sounded a whole lot better than spending the night in a dirty cabin.

The little girl picked up Richard's empty bowl. Going to a bucket of cold, greasy water near the fireplace she dipped it and ran her hand around the inside. Then pulling it out, she took the edge of her ragged skirt and wiped it dry.

"She does a good job with bowls," said her mother with pride. "I be expectin' another one. The old man wants a boy this time."

"You're going to have another baby?" asked Mamma.

"Yep. Sometime in the winter. The last two both died, but I got a feelin' about this one." In the dim light of the candles, Mamma sat and listened to the young woman talk. She stopped only long enough to spit into the fire.

Jenny watched and listened. She felt sorry for the young woman who wasn't more than nineteen years old.

"It's been a long day," Mamma said finally. "Could you please show us where we are to sleep?"

Taking a candle to the loft ladder, the woman showed them a dark, low room with a large bed in the center. On the bed was a straw mattress with two dirty, ragged quilts.

"Bedding was washed two, maybe three months ago. Ain't no one been sleeping up her 'cept a couple of men about a week ago. They looked pretty clean. Something like you folks, they were."

More quilts were stacked in a pile in the corner. "That's where the girl sleeps. But if ya get cold, you can cover up with some of 'em. And if it rains ya can shove 'em in the holes in the roof so ya don't get wet." With that she turned with the candle and descended the ladder.

Standing in the darkness, Jenny could hear Mamma sigh. "Just take off your boots and get into bed. Pray to the good Lord that there's no **bedbugs** in these quilts and that it doesn't rain."

Unlacing her boots Mamma dropped them to the floor and crawled into bed. Jenny followed, wondering where Papa would sleep. From the cracks in the floorboards, slivers of light shot into the darkness. Jenny thought about their home in New

York and wondered who was sleeping in her bed now.

Soon Jenny heard Mamma breathing softly. She had already fallen asleep. The place was not very clean, but at least they didn't have to worry about the wolves that were howling again somewhere in the woods.

Jenny was just about to fall asleep when she heard someone climbing the ladder quietly. It must be Papa, she thought. Just then the little girl crawled into the bed beside her. Cuddling close, she put her arm around Jenny and soon the two of them fell fast asleep.

Chapter 10
A Home of Their Own

Early the next morning Jenny rolled over onto a cold, wet spot on the quilt. Sitting up quickly, she soon discovered that the little girl had wet the bed. But the girl was nowhere to be seen. Jenny got up, and put on her boots, lacing them tightly.

Mamma was soon awake. As she got up she felt the wet spot on the quilt and looked at Jenny with surprise.

"It wasn't me," whispered Jenny. "That little girl crawled into bed with us last night. She did that."

Mamma carefully crawled out of bed and straightened her clothes. After she put on her boots, she and Jenny quietly climbed down the ladder from the loft. The cabin was dark and quiet except for the snores of the old man.

Outside the sun was just starting to rise. Mamma and Jenny passed the stable where Papa and Richard were still sleeping. Then they made their way down the trail to the **necessary house**.

When they returned to the cabin Jenny and Mamma washed at the basin on the bench outside. Jenny spied the little girl wandering nearby in the woods. "Look," Jenny pointed. "What do you think she has been doing?"

Mamma shrugged and finished washing. The little girl came closer and watched as Mamma fixed her own hair up in a bun, then helped Jenny braid hers.

When they were finished Mamma motioned for the little girl to come to her. Taking a clean bucket of water, Mamma scrubbed the girl's face as best she could. Using her fingers she combed through the girl's snarled hair and braided it.

When she finished, Mamma scrubbed her own hands and the little girl bounded off into the cabin. "I think she has lice," whispered Mamma to Jenny. "I hope you didn't catch them sleeping so close to her last night." Jenny swallowed hard.

Just then the old man came out of the cabin. He looked at them and frowned. "Ma'am, I know you be tryin' to help, but I'd appreciate it if you don't go filling my girl's head with fancy ideas. We live here in the wilderness. It's hard enough for her ma to get food on the table and keep the cabin clean. Now you want to fill her head with ideas of washin' up and gettin' her hair fixed everyday. There's no time for that kind of nonsense here in the woods."

Shocked, Mamma apologized.

"You'll see how it is soon enough when you get to your settlement. There won't be time for any fancy fixin' for you either," he said as he turned and headed down the path to the necessary house.

Papa and Richard came from the wagon and stretched. Then they began washing.

As Jenny and Mamma entered the cabin the young woman ran to Mamma and gave her a hug. "Thank ya for fixin' up my gal so pretty. She ain't ever shined so well before."

Mamma pulled back in surprise. Jenny felt sorry for the little girl and her mother. They never had anything nice in their lives and probably never would.

Mamma quickly set to work helping in the kitchen. She heated a kettle of water and scrubbed the dishes, table, and benches before they ate. The young woman fried up some ham and potatoes and cut thick slices of fresh bread. "It'd be nice to have women folk around," she said with a sigh.

When it was time to leave, Mamma crawled into the wagon and brought out a small tortoiseshell haircomb and two of Jenny's blue ribbons. Tears came to the young woman's eyes when Mamma gave them to her. Mamma smiled warmly and gave her a hug. Jenny watched, thinking how lucky she was to have a mother who taught her how to take care of herself.

Papa slapped the backs of the horses with the reins and the wagon pulled away from the cabin. Richard and Jenny walked with the dog as Mamma sat up straight in her seat by Papa, looking stronger than she ever had before. Papa often turned and smiled at her.

As they traveled along the trail, Mamma commented how much the rolling land looked like that of New York State.

Papa smiled, "We aren't the only ones that think that. The old man said that the place we are going just had its name changed to Howell."

"That's a town in New York!" said Mamma.

"I have a feeling we will have as many New Yorkers as neighbors here as we did living in New York," said Papa.

As they traveled on for the next three days, Papa often referred to the maps in his book and followed the sun along the trail as it traveled from east to west. Mamma and Papa did their best to keep their spirits high, and Papa often held Mamma's hand. Each night the wolves started howling as soon as darkness came and kept the family from enjoying a peaceful night's sleep.

On the fourth day Papa studied the map and announced, "I believe we are somewhere between fifteen and twenty-five miles of our land." Everyone decided that they should stop as little as possible and try to make it by nightfall.

After going a short distance they came to a wide stream with a plank bridge. Papa didn't trust the wobbly bridge and sent Richard into the stream to test its bottom. Quickly, however, they decided that the stream's current made it too dangerous to cross.

Papa decided the only solution was to unload the wagon, making it lighter so that it would not fall through the bridge. One at a time, Papa and Richard carried boxes and rolled barrels across the bridge, piling them on the high ground on the other side of the stream. Then Papa led the team and wagon slowly across the shaky structure. When he reached the other side safely Jenny, Richard, and Mamma cheered and began the task of reloading the wagon so that they could resume their travel.

In late afternoon they came to a fork in the road that puzzled Papa. While he examined the map Mamma walked a short distance up each trail.

Reporting back she said, "They're both clear. I don't know which one is best."

"When in doubt, always be right," said Papa as he climbed into his seat and directed the horses to the right fork.

As evening set in the trees and brush seemed to close in around the trail. Soon it was so dark they could hardly see their way. Papa lit a lantern and continued to urge the horses slowly down the trail. Jenny, Richard, and the dog rode in the wagon. Jenny nudged Richard and whispered, "What if we're lost and we never find our way out of the wilderness?"

"You keep still," Richard scolded. "Your pa knows what he's doing. He's guessed right all the way from New York, hasn't he?"

For some reason the answer didn't make Jenny feel better. Out of the back of the wagon she could see the stars twinkling. In the distance she could begin to hear the howl of wolves.

Papa continued up the trail until he came to a turnout. Pulling the horses to a halt he hopped down and went ahead with the lantern. Again, the trail split in two different directions. But between the trails was a tall pole with a piece of red cloth tied to the top. Uncertain which trail the pole was meant to mark, Papa decided to again go right.

About a half mile up the trail the ground started to get soft and muddy. The farther they went, the slower the horses pulled. Finally Papa brought the wagon to a halt and stood on the seat, shining the lantern in front of them. There, not more than twenty feet ahead was a watery marsh.

Mamma, who had been sleeping, now stood wide-eyed beside Papa. "I think we best go back. Maybe we should stop for the night, once we are out of the mud."

Papa agreed and carefully began turning the wagon around on the narrow muddy trail. He whipped the horses' backs to force them to follow each of his commands so that the wagon would not roll too far off the trail.

Just as the horses and wagon were finally turned and headed safely away from the marsh, they saw a light ahead of them. The dog was now alert and barked a warning. In a loud voice Papa called out a greeting. The lantern on the trail moved up and down as a signal.

The dog continued to bark until Richard took his hand and held its mouth firmly shut. "At least it's a human voice," said Richard, "and not a ghost." Jenny shivered and elbowed him in the ribs.

As the lantern moved closer, the voice called out again. "It's Fryer!" exclaimed Papa as he stopped the horses and jumped down from the wagon to meet his friend.

Overjoyed Mamma explained to Jenny and Richard, "It's the man who sold us the land."

After they had exchanged greetings, Mr. Fryer explained, "I left a pole with a warning flag so you wouldn't come down this way."

"So this was the trail I wasn't supposed to take," responded Papa.

"I went out to smoke my pipe and just happened to see your wagon lantern trailing along the marsh. I didn't know it was you, but any wagon headed for the marsh at night is in trouble. If you had gone any farther, you'd been up past your hubs in water.

"You're a green one, Case. Looks like I'll be teaching you a lot over the next few years." Fryer laughed and gave Papa a friendly slap on the back.

"Now follow me and we'll give you a hot meal and a chance to wash up," Fryer said as he led them back toward his cabin.

Inside the Fryer house, Mrs. Fryer held her nursing baby with one arm and cooked a meal with the other. She seemed worked out of strength and almost out of temper. The other Fryer children, awakened from their sleep by their late night visitors, lay on the floor and on a bed which filled nearly a third of the small cabin.

When the baby had finished eating Mamma offered to rock him so that Mrs. Fryer was free to finish preparing the meal. Thankful for the offer, Mrs. Fryer soon recovered her good humor. "It will be good to have a woman near," she said with a smile.

That night Jenny and Mamma slept in clean sheets in the Fryer's loft along with their five children. Papa, Richard, and the dog made their beds by the fire on the clean wooden floor.

The next morning the family quickly packed their wagon and followed Fryer to their new homestead. The sun shone brightly as if to greet them. Mamma smiled and hummed. "With all the children nearby," she said to Papa, "I may need to start a little school."

As the path wound through the woods, they passed a small creek. "This creek is on your property, Case, but you won't be needing it for water. There's a well been dug right up close to the cabin."

Jenny was glad to hear that news, knowing it would be easier to pull a bucket from a well than to carry one from the creek.

As they rounded the last curve on the trail there stood a good-sized cabin with a tall stick chimney. "Here she is," said Fryer with pride. "I didn't tell you no story, did I, Case? This cabin is really something!" He slapped Papa on the back.

"It's something all right," whispered Mamma.

The cabin looked lonely in its small clearing. Although it was larger than many they had seen, it had been sitting for some time without anyone to tend to it. A door with leather hinges hung sagging and open. There was a well a short distance from the door, just as Fryer had said.

Mamma slid down from the wagon and slowly entered the cabin. The cabin had large window openings covered with oilskin material. The oilskin coverings, now worn and ragged, flapped in the breeze.

Fryer accompanied the family as they examined their new home. "It's a fair-looking cabin, Case. It will do your family well."

There were two rooms on the ground floor, separated by a wall that had boards so badly joined that Jenny could see through the gaps. Beneath the main room there was a crude cellar. Its door lay open on the floor, showing the cellar's mud and clay walls.

"Don't you go worrying. I made sure the bear was driven out last week," teased Fryer.

Papa examined the walls of the cabin. They were made of strong logs that had been roughly squared and notched to each other at their ends. The cracks between them were filled with clay.

Above the main rooms was a loft with a shaky-looking ladder. Jenny carefully climbed up and peered at what would be her new bedroom.

"As you can see," said Fryer, "the door will need fixing."

"Well, it looks like I'll be doing that first," Papa said to Mamma who nodded, still in shock.

"At least we have a fine wooden floor," offered Richard, hoping to make Mamma feel better.

"And lots of windows," added Jenny.

"Over here, you got yourself a **sideboard**," said Mr. Fryer as he pointed to a few boards nailed together in the form of a table and supported by the wall. In the center of the room, lying on its side, was another small table. The chairs, four in number, were also scattered about on their sides. On the mantel above the fireplace sat two candlestick holders made from ears of Indian corn.

"Well," said Papa as he swallowed hard and tried to hide his disappointment, "It has possibilities."

Mamma righted a chair and sat down, wondering what they would do first.

"It has a stink about it," Richard blurted out.

"Hush, Richard," said Papa.

"It's nothing a little hot water and soap can't take care of," said Fryer as he headed for the door. "I'll be back tomorrow to show you around the land. How about I take your team with me and feed and water them in my barn. When you get settled, we'll have a **barn raising** for you."

Papa waved to Fryer, picked up another chair, and sat silently beside Mamma. He didn't know what to say. He had been led to believe that the cabin would be much better than this. For the first time since they had begun the journey, he did not know what to do.

Mamma looked at Papa's troubled face and smiled. "Well, husband, I don't know what we're doing sitting. Time's a-wasting. There's work to be done." She stood up and started giving instructions.

"Richard, go bring in some wood so I can boil water for scrubbing. Jenny, I'll need my kitchen barrel and broom. Husband, let's just hope the land is better than the cabin." Papa scratched his head, looked at Mamma, and hoped the same thing.

Richard soon came in with an armload of wood. The dog followed. "Richard," said Mamma. "For now the dog is welcome into the house. But once the barn is built, she will be sleeping there. A house is no place for a dog."

Jenny looked at Richard who hung his head and nodded, "Yes, ma'am."

Mamma then turned to Papa who had started cleaning out the fireplace, removing burned logs and ashes. "Save the ashes," she instructed. "I'll be needing them to make lye for soap."

Papa scooped the ashes into a small empty barrel that sat beside the fireplace. "I had better check the chimney. Looks like the birds have made themselves a home up there."

"Let me look," insisted Richard. He crawled up into the fireplace and stood in the chimney. "There's something up here all right. I can't see daylight." He reached up the dark hole and felt something blocking the chimney.

Papa handed the broom to Richard who used the handle to poke up inside the chimney. "I think I got something. Smells funny up here, too, like. . .." Just then the mass that was blocking the chimney gave way, knocking Richard to the floor and covering him with soot and feathers. All around him lay the bodies of a dozen or more dead ducks.

The air was filled with a terrible stench. Mamma and Jenny raced to the door, nearly knocking each other down in their escape into the fresh air. The dog, delighted by the find, picked up a duck and followed them outside.

Richard spit out feathers and dirt as he rolled to his feet. Papa helped brush him off. "It looks like a whole flock of them just aimed down the chimney and got themselves stuck," he said.

Richard carefully crawled back into the fireplace and looked up. "I can see light. The chimney's clean."

Together Richard and Papa cleaned up the mess, putting the mass of dead ducks, feathers, and leaves outside in a pile. The dog helped by carrying the ducks, one at a time, into the woods and burying them in holes known only to her.

Meanwhile Mamma and Jenny attached a new rope to the well crank and started bringing up water.

Papa started a fire in the fireplace and put water on to boil. After several hours of hard work Jenny and Mamma had scrubbed the lower level of the cabin with boiling water and soap and were ready to start on the loft.

Papa found his box of tools and worked on the leather hinges of the door. "At least it will hold for the night if we're careful," he said. "Tomorrow I'll put on the metal hinges that I have packed away in one of our barrels."

Papa moved on to the windows and with Richard's help, carefully reattached the loose oilcloth pieces to the window openings. "We'll be needing new cloth for these windows before winter," said Richard.

With pride Papa announced, "I have window glass packed for that very purpose."

Mamma looked down from the loft with surprise. "Now how did you keep that glass from breaking on this long trip?" she asked.

"The same way you kept that mirror with the gilded frame from breaking," he teased. "I packed it with the clothes in the trunk." Jenny looked at Mamma in surprise, not knowing that Papa had discovered the mirror.

Papa and Richard went back to work. This time they brought in trunks and boxes. "Do you think we should sleep in the wagon tonight?" asked Papa. "It's nearly empty now, so there'll be plenty of room."

"Indeed not," snapped Mamma. "Do you think I have been working myself to the bone so we could sleep in that old wagon again with the wolves and the wild animals? Tonight we will have ourselves a hot meal and a warm bed in our own cabin, even though the warm bed will be on the floor."

Papa smiled at Mamma. "You've got spunk, woman, and that's what I love about you."

Jenny grinned, but Richard turned away in embarrassment.

"What's wrong with you, boy?" teased Papa. "There's nothing better in the world than the love of a good partner and hard work."

Richard turned and went out the door, and Papa followed. Looking back at Mamma he said, "It appears I have a few things to teach that boy." Mamma laughed and looked at Jenny with a big smile.

"Are we really going to have a hot supper tonight?" Jenny asked.

"How about stew? We've got lots of potatoes, carrots, and onions. There's cornmeal, too. I'll make some bread and maybe a cobbler with the honey and dried apples. We have good cold water from our own well. We'll have a feast."

Grateful that they were together in their new home, Jenny began unpacking their dishes. She put them one at a time on the table that was now covered with one of Mamma's starched, white tablecloths.

Supper that night was the best they had eaten since they left their New York farm. Everyone ate and laughed and talked about the next day when Mr. Fryer would return and show them their land.

After supper Jenny washed the dishes while Mamma, Papa, and Richard put down quilts for the night. The dog had already curled up by the fireplace. Outside the cabin darkness had set in and the wolves had already started to howl. "I suppose this is just something we will have to get used to," said Papa as he took off his boots.

"I'm glad Fryer took the horses," he continued. "When we get a barn they'll be safe, but right now they are better off over there." Mamma nodded in agreement.

Gradually the family drifted off to sleep, feeling safe in their cabin in the woods. After a few hours rain began to fall and a cool dampness filled the air. Hearing water drip on the floor, Papa got up to search for leaks in the cabin's roof. He took several **trenchers** and placed them around the cabin to catch the water as it dripped from the timbers.

No sooner had Papa settled back down to his bed than he noticed the dog had gotten up and was pacing the floor. He called to her quietly, but she ignored him. Then she stopped, staring at the door with her hair standing straight up on her back.

Getting up quietly Papa reached for his gun that now hung above the fireplace. He moved softly toward the door. The wolves had stopped their howling, but he could hear them moving outside the cabin.

Richard awoke and quickly came to Papa's side. "The wolves are outside. I think they smell her in here," whispered Papa.

Richard tried to pull the dog back from the door, but she snarled at him. "Let her be!" Papa said. Just then a loud crack and flash of light split the sky. Richard and Papa jumped and the dog started barking wildly.

By this time Jenny was wide awake and sitting up beside Mamma. "What's wrong?" called Mamma.

In the crack between the floor and the door, they saw the paws of a wolf scratching to get into the cabin. Another wolf scraped the door with its paws. Then it pushed its head against the door, shaking its weak hinges.

The dog snapped and snarled. Richard tried to pull her back, but she was too strong. Breaking away she ran from window to window, standing on her back legs and scratching at the oilskins.

"The door," cried Mamma as it shook and rattled in its frame. Papa and Richard held the door with all their might, trying to avoid the sharp claws of the wolf that scratched on the floor at their feet. "Get to the loft," shouted Papa. Jenny and Mamma scrambled up the shaky ladder and looked down from the loft.

Flashes of lightning filled the sky and great crashes of thunder shook the cabin. The dog, crazy with desire to run with the wolves, still scratched at the windows. Finally she tore the oilskin covering, and as lightning flashed she leaped through the rip and disappeared into the night.

Jenny screamed, and Richard ran to the window, looking out through the rip into the dark, wet night. Wild barking and yelping filled the air as the wolves ran from the cabin and followed the dog into the woods.

Papa stepped back from the doorway in exhaustion, just as Richard turned from the window. A panicked look crossed his face. He raced past Papa, threw open the cabin door, and ran out into the darkness. Papa quickly recovered and followed with his gun in hand.

The wind and rain blew in the door. "You stay here," demanded Mamma as she pointed a finger at Jenny. Jenny watched as Mamma slowly climbed down the ladder and crept to the door and peered into the night.

"Richard," she shrieked as the sky lit up and the rain poured down. "Richard!"

After a moment Mamma closed the door and leaned against the wall in shock. She started to shake with sobs.

Just then Papa burst through the door carrying Richard. Jenny quickly climbed down the ladder as Papa lay Richard on the floor beside the fire, covering him with quilts. Mamma recovered and lit the lanterns.

"He tripped over a tree root and banged his head a good one," said Papa.

"My dog, my dog," repeated Richard as he started to come to.

"Papa, what about the dog?" cried Jenny.

Mamma pushed Jenny aside as she lay a wet towel on Richard's head.

Papa stood and went to the window that the dog had jumped through. "Jenny, come give me a hand with this," he said as he prepared to cover the window with an old quilt.

Jenny stood beside Papa and looked out the big hole. The wind and rain whipped through it, soaking the two of them. "What about the dog!" yelled Jenny as tears formed in her eyes.

Chapter 11
The Journey

"What about the dog," cried Jennifer as she rolled over in her bed, burying her tears in her pillow.

"Jennifer. Jennifer." A bright light lit up her room. She opened her eyes and looked up at her father.

"Are you all right, sweetheart?"

Jennifer sat up in her bed and looked around. The old quilt with its pretty pink flowers covered her.

"Are you all right? You were dreaming."

"But—but—I was in the cabin. The dog, the wolves. . .."

"You fell asleep in the rocker upstairs. It was probably the medicine. I had to carry you down-stairs. You know, you're getting too big for that." Daddy smiled and sat down beside Jennifer on the bed.

"But I—I thought I was in the cabin. It was in the wilderness, where there was nothing except trees and wolves."

"You must have been more awake than I thought you were. That was all part of the story from the journal. You must have fallen asleep while I was still reading and it became part of your dream."

"What happened to the dog? Did the wolves kill her? Did she come back?" Jennifer asked anxiously.

"Well, if you had stayed awake you'd have been surprised. That spring she showed up at the cabin with a whole litter of pups. There were five of them. Two of them had two different colored eyes like their mother."

"Really?" said Jennifer. "What happened to Jenny and Richard?"

"Well, that's an interesting story, too. It's not in the journal, but your grandmother told me that Richard stayed with the Cases for about a year. Then he went out west with a group of pioneers that were pushing on into the wilderness.

"Thanks to Jenny and her mother he had learned to read and write and was able to keep in contact with the family. My grandfather told me that he had read some of Richard's old letters. They were from the Illinois country, Wisconsin, Iowa, and finally Missouri.

"You know that buffalo robe up in the trunk? Richard sent it from the prairies to the family. And you know something else? This is really a surprise. Your great-great-great-great-grandmother Jenny was so impressed by Richard and all the things he accomplished that she finally joined him out west and married him."

"Jenny married Richard! She married Richard? I don't believe it. But weren't they brother and sister?"

"No, don't you remember? He joined the family along the canal. He was a foundling, raised in the swamps. He was just rescued by the family."

"But if she married Richard, it would make him my great-great-great-great-grandfather."

Daniel Case smiled and nodded his head. "That's right."

"Daddy, that's why you have red hair. Wow! This is a cool story!"

"You know, after they married and had kids of their own, they returned to Michigan. They lived on the property that belonged to Jenny's parents. In fact, our house is built right on the very spot where the first cabin was built. And this quilt is the one Jenny started for Aunt Emma, but didn't finish until 1837."

"Wow," said Jenny in amazement. "What happened to Aunt Emma and Uncle McKee?"

"According to my grandmother, they had lots of children and spent their life operating boats along the canal.

"You know, one of these days we will have to visit New York and follow along the old canal. I know there are parts of it that can still be seen, weaving its way along the countryside."

"Let's do that!"

Jennifer and her father were so interested in the family stories that neither heard Jennifer's mother when she came into the room. "Looks like you two have been up in the trunk," she said. "Daniel, that old quilt should be dry cleaned before we put it on her bed. There's no telling where it's been."

Jennifer looked at her father and smiled a knowing smile.

"Well, Jennifer fell asleep upstairs in the old rocker while I was reading the journal to her. She was so comfortable wrapped up in the quilt, I just brought her down in it."

"Maybe we should have it cleaned and mounted so you can hang it on your bedroom wall. Would you like that?" asked her mother.

"Oh, that would be great," said Jennifer.

"I don't know if you two are up to it, but I brought home a pizza and movie. And. . .," she turned and reached behind the bedroom door. "This is for you, birthday girl. It's from Daddy and me." Jennifer's mother handed her a large box wrapped in gold foil with a big pink ribbon.

"Were you able to get the right one?" asked Daniel.

"I sure was and it was the last one they had," said her mother. "Jennifer, this is a very special gift and it really isn't something that's meant to be played with. But your father and I thought you were old enough to enjoy it. It will mean even more to you now that you have heard the journal."

Quickly Jennifer untied the pink ribbon and ripped the gold paper from the box. Lifting the lid, she looked inside to see a beautiful, large porcelain doll all dressed in old-fashioned clothes, complete with boots, long skirts, and a pink-flowered sunbonnet.

Jennifer's eyes lit up. "It's Jenny."

"How did you know her name? Her name tag is in the bottom of the box with a little book."

"No, you don't understand. This *is* Jenny. This is the girl who was in my dream—my great-great-great-great-grandmother."

Jennifer's parents smiled, happy that she liked her special doll. But Jennifer knew she was more than just a doll.

Just then Sage flashed through the doorway. The brown and tan ball of energy hopped up on the bed, tearing the wrapping paper and licking Jennifer's face.

"I hope she hasn't been in the house all day. You know a house is no place for a dog."

It was then that Jennifer realized how special Sage was with one blue eye and the other brown.

Territory Talk

ague. A sickness with fever and chills.

aqueduct. Bridge-like structure which carried the canal across rivers.

barn raising. A gathering where neighbors and friends build a barn for someone.

bedbugs. Lice.

bedstead. Frame for a bed.

beholden. To owe someone something. To be grateful for a favor.

belly wobbles. Stomachache.

berm. A bank of earth along the edge of the canal.

blouson. A long blouse that ties at the waist, giving it a full, puffy look.

bounty. A reward for capturing or killing dangerous animals.

bow. The front part of a boat.

carpetbags. Bags made out of carpeting.

cholera epidemic. An outbreak of an infectious disease much like the intestinal flu. Cholera epidemics killed many people in 1832 and 1834.

corduroy road. Road made of logs.

court. To pay attention to and try to get the love of another in order to marry them.

cussing. Swearing.

Da. Dad, father.

dig camps. Temporary camps where the canal workers lived.

drawers. Underwear with long legs.

dry goods. Merchandise such as material and clothing. A dry goods store would not sell groceries or hardware.

emigrants. People who leave one place to settle in another.

feeder creek. Stream, river, or creek that feeds into a canal.

fiddle-footed. Always on the move.

fitful. Restless.

gruel. Thin cereal made by boiling meal in water or milk.

headstrong. Stubborn, unwilling to listen to others.

hoggee. Person, usually a boy, who drives the horses or mules along the towpath.

hotspur. A person who looses his temper easily and acts impulsively. Hothead.

influenza. Flu.

johnnycakes. Cakes made of cornmeal and water or milk and cooked on a griddle.

kin. Relative.

king's ransom. A lot of money.

knitting. Busy work or business.

lassie. Young girl.

malaria. A disease spread by mosquitoes.

mush. Cornmeal boiled in milk or water to make a soft thick mass.

necessary house. Outhouse or outdoor bathroom.

oak openings. Open areas in oak forests where the trees grew so tall and gave so much shade that little else could grow beneath them.

oilcloth. Cotton material treated with oil for waterproofing and often used for tablecloths.

oilskin. Cotton material made waterproof with oil and often used for rain gear.

pilings. Heavy timbers with pointed ends which are driven into the ground.

pocket doors. Doors which slide into an opening or "pocket" in the wall instead of swinging open and closed on hinges.

rooting. Digging or turning up the soil.

runaway. A person that runs away, in this case from slavery.

salt pork. A fatty part of the pork that is cured with salt, much like bacon.

second land. Land previously owned and partially cleared by another.

shift. A slip worn under a dress or skirt.

shucking dance. A dance held after a shucking bee which is a gathering of people to husk corn.

sideboard. A long narrow table which is attached to the wall and is often used for dining.

sop. Soup or broth.

speculator. Person who buys and sells for a profit.

spinster. An older woman who has never married.

stern. The back end of a boat.

stowaway. Someone who hides aboard a boat, usually to get free transportation.

tick. A mattress cover, sometimes called a bed tick.

tiller. A bar or handle for turning the rudder of a boat.

towline. A rope connecting the canal boat to the team of mules or horses.

towpath. Path along the edge of the canal where the horse or mule team walked while towing the boat.

trenchers. Shallow wooden bowls.

urchin. Mischievous youngster.

vendue. Public auction, in this case where the settlement paid the lowest bidder to take a poor person to live with them in exchange for work.